IMAGES
of America

FORT DUPONT

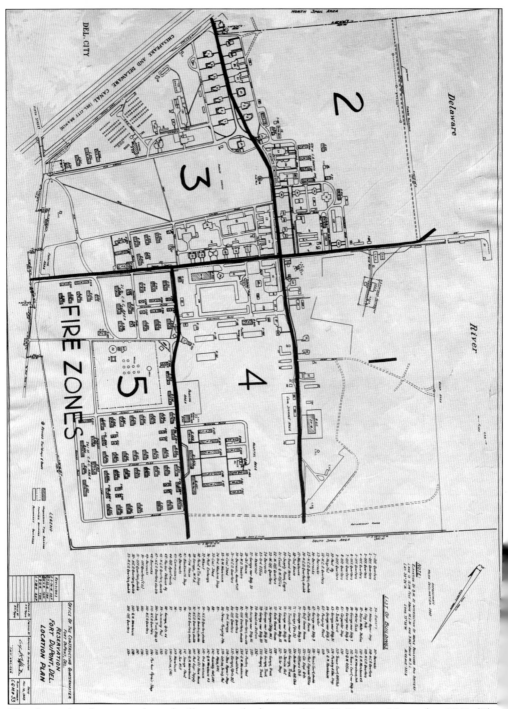

The above sketch, oriented north, illustrates the layout of Fort DuPont in November 1941. (Pla
by A.W. Poppe; National Archives.)

ON THE COVER: Soldiers and civilians pose with the Fort DuPont push ball outside of the po
exchange and gymnasium building sometime in the 1940s. (Delaware Historical Society.)

IMAGES
of America

FORT DUPONT

Brendan Mackie, Peter K. Morrill,
and Laura M. Lee

ARCADIA
PUBLISHING

Published by Arcadia Publishing
Charleston, South Carolina

Printed in the United States of America

Library of Congress Control Number: 2011927486

For all general information, please contact Arcadia Publishing:
Telephone 843-853-2070
Fax 843-853-0044
E-mail sales@arcadiapublishing.com
For customer service and orders:
Toll-Free 1-888-313-2665

Visit us on the Internet at www.arcadiapublishing.com

*To Lee Jennings—cohort, colleague, partner in crime, source
of inspiration, and loyal friend—you are missed.*

The quartermaster storehouse (Building 43) was built in 1906 following standard plan No. 91-D. This load-bearing masonry structure, complete with a raised basement, served as the post commissary in the 1930s and 1940s. Currently, this building is well preserved and serves as the Surplus Property warehouse, which is open to the public every Tuesday and Wednesday. (National Archives.)

CONTENTS

ACKNOWLEDGMENTS

Why preserve historic buildings? There is a compelling argument for adaptive reuse of sites like Fort DuPont. It is the pinnacle of recycling. Don Rypkema in *The Economics of Rehabilitation* stated:

> Historic preservation is a rational and effective economic response to overconsumption. To make a new brick today to build a building on a site where there is already a building standing steals from two generations. It steals from the generation that built the brick originally by throwing away their asset before its work is done, and it steals from a future generation by using increasingly scarce natural resources today that should have been saved for tomorrow.

We give many thanks to all who have helped to preserve Fort DuPont and its story. This work would not be possible without the support of many. The Architectural Survey and Evaluation completed by the University of Delaware's Center for Historic Architecture and Engineering provided essential information, and the Coastal Defense Study Group's *Coast Defense Journal* was invaluable as well.

The Fort Delaware Society graciously shared images from its collections. Delaware State Parks' Cultural Resources Unit, namely George Contant, opened files to provide volumes of information. The Delaware Historical Society, Delaware Public Archives, National Archives, Army Corps of Engineers, and Delaware Military Heritage and Education Foundation all contributed to this work. Most of all, many thanks to those, living and gone, who had the vision to save personal photographs, menus, football programs, and all sorts of mementos of life at Fort DuPont.

On a frigid day back in 1992, Lee Jennings, a Delaware state parks historian, dragged me on a walk through Fort DuPont. I marveled at his bursting exuberance, for before I had passed by this place many days without a second thought. Somehow, in just an hour or so, he made it magically come alive with his passion and his vision for what could be. Lee's tireless pursuit of saving history has fostered the preservation of not only Fort DuPont but also many other pieces of history in Delaware. He hooked many of us in his relentless pursuit to save history. Sadly, he passed away suddenly, long before we were ready for him to go. On behalf of all of us, thank you, Lee. History thanks you, too.

—Laura M. Lee

Bonnie Bonner Rorabaugh, pictured at left, recalls growing up at Fort DuPont: "Living at Fort du Pont for 13 years as a young girl was not always filled with fun and games. There were happy times, but some sad times too, and even a few embarrassing times. Overall, though, those were years that I will always treasure for the friends, the experiences, and the memories of growing up on a military installation. The most poignant memories of all would be the parades, the military band music, and the bugler at night sounding those haunting notes of Taps." (Photograph by Violet Bonner.)

INTRODUCTION

Fort DuPont, located between Delaware City and the Chesapeake and Delaware Canal, has often been overlooked in the history annals because of its neighbor, Fort Delaware. But while the island neighbor is infamous for its role as a Civil War prison camp, Fort DuPont played a longer and more significant role in the history of Delaware River defenses. The post was named for Rear Adm. Samuel Francis Du Pont, a Delaware resident and key player in the blockade of southern ports during the Civil War. While it was officially designated as "Fort DuPont" in 1899, its story begins more than 100 years earlier.

The post was constructed on the Reeden Point tract granted to a Henry Ward in 1675, with his land beginning at a "bevor Damme standing by a Thickety Swampe." During the American Revolution, the Reeden Point Farm Company did business in marsh hay and horses, both valuable commodities in wartime. Ships pulled up to the riverbank and were directly loaded with hay for transport to Philadelphia. The land was always a key defensive position for the Delaware River, and soldiers lay in wait for anticipated British attacks in 1778. Captain Aiken, an innkeeper from Newark, Delaware, sheltered the small continental navy in a large ditch somewhere on the site. Aiken awaited an expected attack by British troops that never came. Plans during the War of 1812 that never came to reality also called for gunboats and hotshot batteries putting out heated cannonballs to set enemy wooden ships ablaze.

In 1816, in response to the War of 1812, Congress authorized the Engineer Corps to create a permanent system of national defense. A British blockading squadron that had set up off the entrance to the Delaware Bay prompted attention to the defense of the Delaware and Chesapeake Bays. America feared a war fought on home soil, and President Monroe was spurred to action. He tasked the Army Corps of Engineers to create a plan for coastal defense of the country, and as part of that, a three-tiered redoubt-style fortification was proposed on the Delaware City coastline. After the War of 1812, improvements in artillery capabilities and building technology led to the construction of new fortifications, which could be placed at greater distances from the cities being defended. New sites, such as Fort DuPont also made use of the local topography, in this case marshland, to force enemy troops to land a significant distance from their target and slow their progress.

The Reedy Point site, nestled between Delaware City farmland to the north and marshland to the south, met those requirements. Forty miles south of Philadelphia, the site allowed a clear line of fire downstream. But a devastating fire at Fort Delaware in 1831 may have possibly put this project on the side burner, as the military focused resources on the island post. For whatever reason, the government did not begin construction of a mainland fortification until the Civil War.

On December 23, 1861, Brig. Gen. Joseph Totten wrote, "Besides these preparations, application is now before Congress for a grant of money to commence a new fort opposite to Fort Delaware and for the means of increasing the defensive capacity of Fort Mifflin, as well as completing the barrack accommodations of Fort Delaware." In that year, $200,000 was requested for a "new fort opposite Fort Delaware on Delaware shore."

Fort Delaware's armament included 10-inch guns, but its 1840s design did not support the placement of the more imposing 15-inch Rodman guns. The mainland site was ideal for the placement of these formidable weapons. In September 1863, the government formally seized 20 acres of land on the site from Lt. Clement Reeves, 5th Delaware Infantry. A 10-gun battery, designed by Lt. Col. Henry Brewerton in 1863, was constructed on the site to support nearby Fort Delaware, as well as guard the western channel of the river. Together with Fort Delaware, the new 10-gun battery helped protect the shipping channels of the Delaware River and the eastern mouth of the greatly important Chesapeake and Delaware Canal.

The mainland fortress had several names during its infancy. An 1864 reference to the site as "Fort Reynolds" appears in a letter home by Sgt. Bishop Crumrine. A Pittsburgh soldier based at Fort Delaware, Sergeant Crumrine was sent to the mainland to oversee the new battery. His letters detail his change of "base of operations" from Fort Delaware to Fort Reynolds, sent "with 32 men to garrison this Fort and to assist the Engineer Department, to mount the cannon." Two months later, Crumrine changed his letter headings from "Fort Reynolds" to "Ten Gun Battery" and speaks of the expansion of his mainland garrison, Independent Battery G, Pittsburgh Heavy Artillery. Before the end of the war, only a few of Fort Reynolds' guns were mounted, and by 1870 the fortification was abandoned.

In 1871, sixty-two acres were transferred from Clement Reeves to the federal government, this time legitimately purchased for $18,000. Just a year later, construction began on a new and larger Twenty Gun Battery on the site, using brick and experimental concrete. Under Lt. Col. John Kurtz, construction began on this new series of emplacements. Fortifications of this period made use of the lessons learned in the Civil War. They included brick and concrete gun emplacements, bomb proofs, and magazines all protected behind an earthen slope to deaden incoming projectiles. While plans were quite grandiose, Twenty Gun Battery never received its full complement of weaponry and had only three operable guns. During this time period, it was often referred to as "the Fort Opposite Fort Delaware" because of its location across the river from Fort Delaware. A new wharf and extensive dyke system were also constructed, but funding appropriations eventually dried up. Kurtz, who was involved in many other river and harbor projects, left to work on the foundation of the Washington Monument in 1876, and with his death in 1877, the Delaware project ground to a halt. Weather played a huge part in the demise of the project as well. High waters resulting from 1877 and 1878 storms struck the area, causing extensive damage to the works. Twenty Gun Battery, which did not officially receive all of its guns or even a formal name, never saw full completion. Twenty years went by before the Army again placed a major focus on mainland defense in Delaware City.

In the following years, public and Congressional concern was once again raised concerning the state of American defenses, which had languished during peacetime. Rapid advances in weaponry in the space of just 30 years produced guns that could fire projectiles with remarkable accuracy and four times the weight and distance of the Civil War smoothbores. In 1885, Pres. Grover Cleveland assembled a special board headed by William C. Endicott to review coastal defenses nationwide and make recommendations for improvements. The Endicott Board recommended creation of a modern generation of seacoast defenses to keep up with the advances in military technology. New fortifications were a radically different design than their Civil War–era predecessors. The cost of implementing the plans far exceeded the government's capacity to finance the effort, however. The projected tab for the Delaware City site amounted to $3.8 million. Construction of a substantially modified version of the plan began in 1897.

At the outset of the Spanish-American War, construction on the new batteries of the three forts was still underway, leaving the river mostly unprotected. In response, three grand groups of torpedoes, otherwise known as mines, were laid in the river in late April 1898. The western channel group was controlled via a mining casemate that was constructed just north of Twenty Gun Battery at Fort DuPont. The system was fraught with problems, including leakage, broken mooring lines, electrical connections, and ship strikes. In 1897, the chief of engineers authorized the new construction at the mainland post, and on July 22, 1899, Army General Order 134 officially designated the site as "Fort DuPont." The fortification would eventually boast two 8-inch disappearing guns, two 12-inch guns on barbette mounts, sixteen 12-inch mortars, and rapid-fire guns in forward positions.

The new defenses of the Delaware River now relied on the modern technologies of steel breech-loading artillery. Fort Delaware was modified to mount three of these new 12-inch disappearing guns, but simply refitting the antiquated Civil War–era fort was not sufficient to protect the river. The new fortifications to be constructed were on the Delaware Shore near the unfinished Twenty Gun Battery, as well as directly across the river on the New Jersey side where another 1870s battery had been left incomplete. These two new fortifications would become known as Fort DuPont and Fort Mott, respectively. Fort Mott housed the main long-range rifle batteries of 10-inch and 12-inch disappearing guns. The positions on Pea Patch Island and Fort Mott had a longer view down river because of the topography of the area and were thus selected for the long-range rifles. Fort DuPont, however, received the mortars that were capable of firing over the land forming the bend in the river, and thus they provided support to the rifle batteries in New Jersey.

These larger, more powerful weapons also required more soldiers to operate them, changing the face of the installation radically. Compared to the Civil War gun crews of five or six men, these weapons called for crews of anywhere from 12 to 30 soldiers, not to mention the additional support personnel required. Fort DuPont grew to encompass a larger tract of land in order to provide room for the various service, residential, and administrative buildings. Rapidly it began to take shape as a formal military post, with barracks, a parade field, and various support structures. Similar to many other Endicott-era posts, it was organized with two main road arteries and numerous secondary streets. Fort DuPont grew to become the new headquarters for the Harbor Defenses of the Delaware.

The beginning of World War I signaled a change for Fort DuPont as the war focused attention on homeland defenses. Battleships now carried dramatically increased firepower and in addition, the airplane was first successfully used in combat during the Great War. The older Endicott-era defenses provided no cover from airplane attack, and the guns had become outmatched by their naval brethren. During this time period, Fort DuPont was partially disarmed. Eight mortars from Batteries Best and Rodney were removed for defenses on Hawaii and California in 1914. Safety and stability concerns played a role in this decision, leaving two mortars in each of the four pits. Later, in 1917, the eight-inch disappearing guns were removed from Battery Gibson because they were too light in caliber to be affective against modern warships. The following year, the 12-inch barbette guns of Battery Rodney were removed. In the year 1918, the Army tried to remedy the post's inability to ward off an aerial attack. Antiaircraft gun batteries were placed at several locations in Delaware, including two 3-inch guns placed atop the old Twenty Gun Battery. Over the coming years, as the batteries were placed on caretaker status, Fort DuPont's role gradually changed from defender to trainer. It became the headquarters of the 1st Engineer Regiment and continued as the headquarters of the Harbor Defenses of the Delaware.

World War II further transformed Fort DuPont, and it acquired a new purpose. Preparation for global war replaced coastal defense as the main goal. On December 7, 1941, after the attack on Pearl Harbor, the fort received an emergency message from the war department: "Set Condition Zero." Not long after, units from Fort DuPont were moved to the new Fort Miles on Cape Henlopen, which then became the new headquarters for the Harbor Defenses of the Delaware. At this southern location, the guns (some with ranges close to 26 miles) could focus on potential enemies at sea. Fort DuPont's role now was that of a critical training facility as only two rapid-fire guns and a complement of mortars remained of the old coast artillery weapons. Soldiers were schooled in communications, chemical warfare, combat, and weapons, among others. The XIII Army Corps, a unit that came closer to Berlin than any other, spent 18 months at the site training for its role in the war. Scores of new buildings were constructed that were intended as temporary or mobilization-type buildings.

The fort also assumed another new role—that of a prisoner of war camp. Thousands of captured German soldiers were brought to the post after North Africa fell to the Allies. One of many such camps in the United States, the prisoners spent their time learning English, working on nearby farms, and performing maintenance work. At the close of the war, the crew members of the German submarine *U-858* were received at the post after they surrendered at Fort Miles.

The war's end marked the last page of Fort DuPont's illustrious military career. Declared surplus, the property was given to the State of Delaware. The site was parceled off to serve a variety of state agencies, including the Governor Bacon Health Center, Division of Purchasing, Delaware Army National Guard, and the state's civil defense headquarters. Time took its toll on the historical buildings, exacerbated by a lack of funding. It did not go unnoticed by citizens. Bill Frank, a columnist for the *Wilmington Morning News* brought attention to its plight through his columns and was later joined in his passion by Leah Roedel, a tireless advocate for parks. Roedel's passion for preserving open spaces and parkland for future generations made her a relentless, inspirational advocate for the creation of a park on the site. Spending 10 years lobbying various organizations and politicians, she succeeded in helping to create Fort DuPont State Park on part of the property, encompassing a large number of the historical structures. Decades after Frank had first written about the degradation of the former military post, on March 4, 1992, approximately 185 acres of the Governor Bacon Health Center became Fort DuPont State Park, thanks largely to the efforts of Roedel and Frank. Shortly after, another 140 acres were added to bring the total to 324 acres. Unfortunately, by the time parts of the post became a state park many of the significant structures had been torn down by their supposed caretakers. Even after the post's inclusion as a state park, many buildings continue to feel the ill effects of time and lack of maintenance. Despite the desperate condition of many structures on the post, steps have been made in the right direction with the aim to bring people back to the fort and encourage its adaptive reuse and preservation. A boat ramp and hiking trails became a reality, along with renovation of the tennis courts and a basketball court.

Much of the former Fort DuPont still remains outside of the park, and historical structures are in need of costly stabilization and restoration. A resident curatorship program under the Delaware State Parks aims to engage public assistance in restoration of the grand buildings. In 1999, Fort DuPont was placed in the National Register of Historic Places in order to help protect its surviving cultural resources. Community support for preservation of the post is growing, supplemented by interpretive programs, such as a gun battery tour, walking tours, themed military weekends, and the use of the post for local soccer leagues, baseball clubs, and other recreational activities. Children of officers who grew up on the post in the early part of the 20th century are now older adults, happy to share their mementos, photographs, and stories of life on the post. Their oral histories help to further the interpretation of the site. If the walls could talk, they would resound with the grand stories about the vibrant community that was at Fort DuPont, and we will attempt to tell some of these stories with the photographs and memories left behind.

On August 1, 1936, band members of the 1st Engineer Regiment gather on the parade field near the post commanders house at Fort DuPont. The commanding officer of the band is Lt. B.B. Bruce (sixth from left) and the bandmaster is Warrant Officer Rudolph L. Klenik (seventh from left). Klenik and his family lived in the oldest house on post (Building 23), and they were neighbor to the Bonner family. Seated next to Klenik is S.Sgt. Fay G. Lewis, senior trumpeter and the father of Neil Lewis. The Lewis family lived on Battery Lane across from the post commissary and bakery. (Photograph by E.O. Goldbeck; Fort Delaware Society.)

One

THE BATTERY AT DELAWARE CITY
1815–1892

While construction took place on the star-shaped version of Fort Delaware, the board of engineers made plans to also fortify the mainland. An 1821 operations summary estimated that construction would cost $347,257. The board's estimate was nearly $100,000 more than the Fort Delaware quote, due to the works required to secure the approaches on the land front. But construction on the Delaware shore did not take place for another 40 years.

In 1864, Lt. Col. Henry Brewerton's plans for the Ten Gun Battery became reality. It was a pentagonal, redoubt-style structure that was almost 250 feet in width. The fortification included a heavily reinforced magazine, parade ground, kitchen, and quarters. The earthen and frame construction complete with the trench and palisade made the fort more resilient to the new rifled cannon fire than its masonry predecessors. Six 10-inch guns and four 15-inch guns were to be installed, some of which were capable of firing a 300-pound projectile over 2.5 miles.

Sgt. Bishop Crumrine, posted at Fort Delaware with the Pittsburgh Heavy Artillery, was reassigned to Delaware City to establish a garrison there. Letters to his brother detail life at Fort Reynolds or "the battery." Crumrine wrote:

> You can hardly imagine how busy I have been since I have been at this place and how nice I have made the place look. Six great large guns mounted and painted off nice, the grass growing nice and green on the parapet and magazine . . . The quarters all fixed up nice . . . large stove in the kitchen, great pile of coal in the coal house, three months rations in the storehouse for 50 men . . . if you remember that I had to haul all the gun Carriages all the way from the wharf by hand, which is over a quarter of a mile. And that the guns we mounted on them weighed from 7 to 25 tons you can nearly imagine how busy I have been.

By 1870, the battery was abandoned for a new 20-gun emplacement. But the plans never saw completion, and by the turn of the century, a new generation of fortification was imminent.

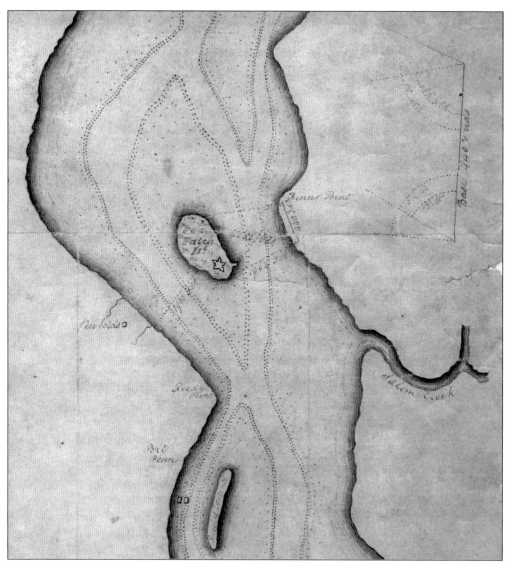

Forty miles south of Philadelphia, Pennsylvania, and situated along the Delaware River, a narrow bend in the channel was recognized early on by military engineers as a formidable location for coastal defense. On the Delaware side, Newbold's Landing (later Delaware City) was chosen as the eastern entrance for the man-made Chesapeake and Delaware Canal. The land south toward Reedy Point was proposed as a fort. Pea Patch Island was selected as an optimal location for Fort Delaware. Finns Point eventually completed the trifecta as a supporting defense site. The above map dates around 1815, which is the same year a young Samuel Francis Du Pont began his career in the US Navy. A century later, the *Fort DuPont Flashes* reported, "It is fitting that the fort should bear the honored name of DuPont, a name almost synonymous with National Defense. The founder of the line, Pierre Samuel du Pont de Nemours, a French statesman, was a friend of the Revolutionary cause. A son Victor du Pont was Captain of one of the Delaware companies in the war of 1812. A younger son, Irénée established and developed the manufacture of powder near Wilmington. Samuel Francis Du Pont, in whose honor the post is named, served conspicuously in the Navy." The article stated further, "In all ways the military defense of the state and nation has enlisted the loyalty of members of this family." (National Archives.)

One of the first to capitalize the family surname, Samuel Francis Du Pont (1803–1865) was born at Bergen Point, New Jersey, the son of Victor Marie du Pont. He spent his childhood in Brandywine Hundred (Wilmington, Delaware) on the estate of his uncle Eleuthère Irénée du Pont, the founder of the notable gunpowder company. At age 12, Samuel Francis secured an appointment as a midshipman by Pres. James Madison. In December 1815, he boarded the *Franklin* and embarked down the Delaware River, passing the site that one day would bear his name. (Delaware Historical Society.)

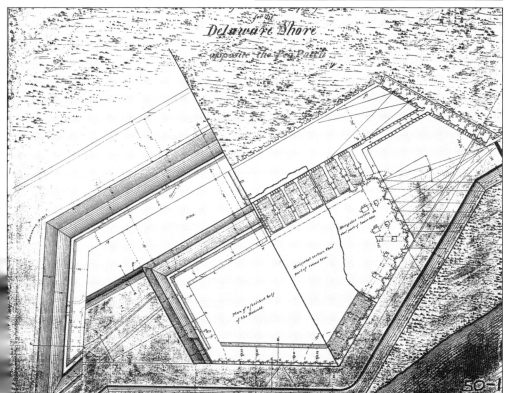

Plan of the Redoubt projected for the Delaware Shore" dates around 1819 and shows the terrain eatures surrounding the third-system fortification. The marshy nature is due to the proximity f the Delaware River. To properly cover sectors of fire, the fort was planned to be close to the marshy riverbank. (National Archives.)

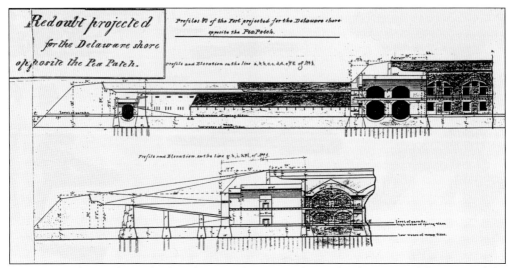

This sectional view shows the foundation and casemate layout for the proposed fort. One of the key characteristics in third-system fortifications is the use of casemates as building blocks. Note the grillage and piles visible under the scarp walls. An extensive foundation was required because of the unstable ground. On February 7, 1821, the board of engineers reported: "In the Delaware, the fort on the Pea Patch island, and one [proposed] on the Delaware shore opposite, defend the water passage as far below Philadelphia as localities will permit: They force an enemy to land forty miles below the city to attack it by land, and thus afford time for the arrival of succors [. . .] The two projected forts will also have the advantage of covering the canal destined to connect the Chesapeake with the Delaware[.]" (National Archives.)

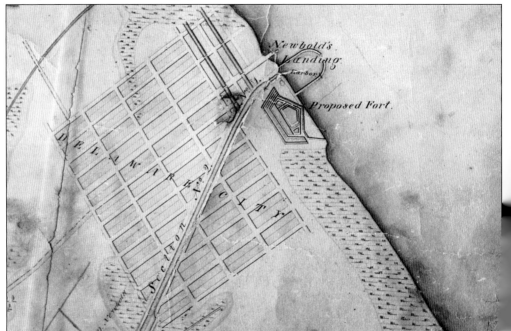

This c. 1829 map shows the geographic relationship between Delaware City, the proposed fort, and the canal. The town streets below the canal never developed, and the land remained for farming. (Delaware State Parks.)

Wilmington Nov. 22nd 1862.

Lieut. Clement Reeves
Delaware City, Del.

Dear Sir,

I herewith enclose your commission from the War Department. Please have your Oath duly executed according to the directions prescribed on the face of your commission, and returned to the Adj't. Genl.

Yours Very Respectfully,
H. S. McComb
Colonel 5th Reg. Del. Vols.
pr. P.R. Craig
Cpt. & A.D.M.

In November 1862, Clement Reeves was commissioned as a lieutenant in Company H, 5th Delaware Infantry. On September 1, 1863, Reeves's nearby property (worth 62 acres) was seized by the government for use as a military reservation. (Letter by Col. Henry McComb; Fort Delaware Society.)

Lt. Col. Henry Brewerton (1801–1879), an Army engineer, designed Ten Gun Battery in 1863. That year, the *Philadelphia Inquirer* reported, "It will occupy about six acres of ground. It will be quite a formidable work, and fully able to sink almost any vessel-of-war coming up the Delaware. Lt. W.H. Hutton is the engineer of construction; Reuben Anderson has the supervision of the wood-work and Clement Reeves is general superintendent. It is expected that it will be completed by Christmas." After the war, Colonel Brewerton, a graduate of the US Military Academy, retired as a brevet brigadier general and spent his last years in Delaware. (US Army Military History Institute.)

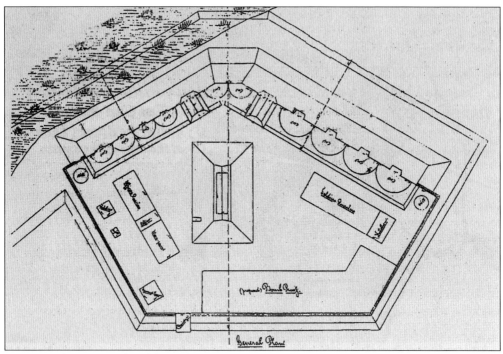

On November 7, 1863, the *Philadelphia Inquirer* reported, "A Ten Gun Battery is being constructed by the government on land purchased of Clement Reeves, Esq., near Delaware City, on the Delaware River. It is to have two faces. Six of the guns are to be 10 inches and four 15 inches, [and] the magazine [will be] bomb-proof and [there will be] bomb-proof protection for the garrison." (Plan by Lt. Col. Henry Brewerton; National Archives.)

In August 1864, at 23 years old, Sgt. Bishop Crumrine, Independent Battery G, Pittsburgh Heavy Artillery, was ordered to take charge of the Ten Gun Battery. During the war, Sergeant Crumrine wrote he "weighed 170 pounds," did "not want to wear government shoes," and preferred "pants made of dark blue" which "will not get dirty as quick." According to compiled military records, Crumrine had blue eyes, dark brown hair, a fair complexion, and stood 5 feet and 11 inches. This unidentified soldier, photographed at Fort Delaware in 1863, matches the profile of Sergeant Crumrine. This soldier even dons an emblem similar to the fraternity pin requested by Crumrine in a wartime letter. A modern restaging of this image (using the exact model chair, same camera angle, and comparable subject) offers favorable circumstantial evidence. (Photograph by John L. Gihon.)

On September 15, 1864, Sgt. Bishop Crumrine wrote, "I have been working hard all day hauling gun carriages and chassises from Delaware City to the Fort. I just swing them under large wheels, and then 25 or 30 men can easily haul them up." He further writes the "fortification is not properly a Fort but rather a water battery. Situated just across the river from Fort Delaware on the Delaware City side, it has five sides. The two longest sides, being next to the river, is a heavy breast work, on which six 10-inch and four 15-inch guns are [to be] mounted." Crumrine's letter, right, further describes progress made at Ten Gun Battery. (Washington and Jefferson College.)

Ten Gun Battery
Near Delaware City
Nov. 28th 1864.

Dear Brother.

I received your letter a few days ago. but have been too busy to answer it. You can hardly imagine how busy I have been since I have been at this place. and how nice I have made the place look. Six great large guns mounted and painted off nice. the grass growing nice and green on the parapet and magazine. the parade all gravelled off nice. The quarters all fixed up nice. large stoves in them. Large stove in the kitchen. great pile of coal in the coal house. Three months ration in the store house. for 50 men &c. Now if you remember that I had to haul all the gun Carriages all the way from the wharf. by hand. which is over a quarter of a mile. and that the guns we mounted on them weigh from 7 to 25 tons you can nearly imagine how busy I have been

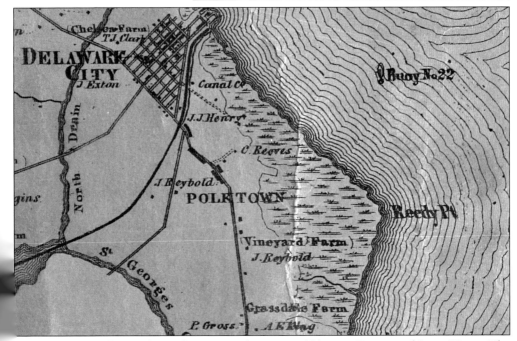

A local map, dated 1860, shows the property locations of Clement Reeves and James Henry. The Ten Gun Battery was close to Henry's peach orchard along Reeves's northernmost boundary. (Map by D.J. Lake and S.N. Beers; Fort Delaware Society.)

Brig. Gen. Albin Francisco Schoepf commanded Fort Delaware, which included the battery at Delaware City. According to General Schoepf, "2nd Lieut. Henry Warner Jr. is hearby relieved from duty as Post Adjutant, and will immediately take charge of the Water Battery at Delaware City, Del. He will select such men as may be necessary for the Garrison, and will make weekly reports to these Head Quarters of the condition of his command." On November 28, 1864, Sgt. Bishop Crumrine wrote that General Schoepf "sent a lieutenant over to take command. Not because I had not done my duty properly, but because he said I had too much to do for the pay I got, and that there was too much responsibility resting upon the narrow shoulders of a sergeant. I am very well pleased as he is one of our lieutenants and one of the best we have too, but he might as well have come and helped me do the work at first." (Photograph by Webster and Bro.)

In May 1864, Lt. Henry Warner (center) sits among a group of unidentified soldiers from Independent Battery G, Pittsburgh Heavy Artillery. The majority stationed at the battery were new recruits who joined the unit in 1863 and 1864. (Photograph by John L. Gihon; Delaware State Parks.)

On December 30, 1864, Pvt. Alexander J. Hamilton (right) wrote in his journal, "went to Delaware City [and] did my shopping. John [Lorentz] came over, took 2 or 3 drinks, went out to the battery, [and] then [we] came back to town and filled ourselves with whiskey." Both soldiers were members of Independent Battery G, Pittsburgh Heavy Artillery. Private Hamilton was stationed at Fort Delaware while Private Lorentz was assigned to the water battery. (Photograph by Roshon Studio; Fort Delaware Society.)

The Roshon Studio

AMONG THE PEACHES.

GATHERING THE FRUIT.

On May 25, 1865, Sergeant Crumrine wrote that the battery "is a nice place now, all the 10-inch guns are mounted and the 15-inch [guns] are on the Wharf. The grass is long and green, and I keep it trimmed as nice as a posy bed. The government property is all fenced in, and I am now thinking how I can get lime to whitewash the fence. Our garden is flourishing peas a foot high, onions, and potatoes in abundance. Henry Champ, gardener." James Henry's peach orchard was located just north and offered a surreal backdrop for the auxiliary battery. (Delaware State Parks.)

On June 18, 1865, Independent Battery G, Pittsburgh Heavy Artillery, was mustered out of the Army and traveled home via Philadelphia. Five days later, while also in Philadelphia, Adm. Samuel Francis Du Pont suddenly passed away after 50 years of military service. The famous naval officer was buried in the Du Pont family cemetery in Greenville, Delaware. (Photograph by Matthew Brady; Delaware Historical Society.)

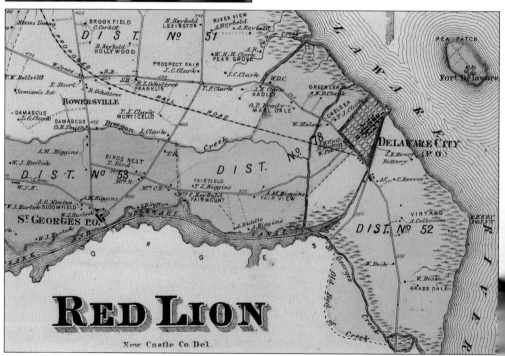

In 1868, the battery appears on the Red Lion Hundred map, which displays the close proximity of the battery to the farm of James Henry. The same year, the water battery was abandoned and the heavy guns were shipped elsewhere. (Map by Pomeroy and Beers Company; Delaware Historical Society.)

Battery Delaware Shore, Southern pack, from Southwest
Sept. 7-1892

In September 1871, the federal government bought the original reservation for $18,000. The same year, construction began on a permanent battery located south of the original work. Still without a real name, she was simply known as Twenty Gun Battery. (Fort Delaware Society.)

The photographer stood atop the southern magazine to capture this 1892 photograph. These guns were manufactured in 1866 by the Cyrus Alger & Company of Boston, Massachusetts. (Fort Delaware Society.)

Battery—Delaware Shore Opposite Ft. Delaware, Southern part Looking Southward—from top of central Magazine—Sept. 6 1892

In 1875, a lack of funding slowed construction which eventually ended within two years. In 1877 and 1878, storms caused considerable damage on the government reservation, destroying the dike and ruining temporary structures and the fence line that encompassed the site. In the 1880s, limited funds were allocated for minor repairs only. The above photograph shows two 10-inch Rodmans (one barely visible) and a pile of bricks (right) amongst the overgrown battery. (Fort Delaware Society.)

In 1892, a mine casemate was constructed near the northern flank of the permanent battery. The estimated cost was $114,250 for mine defenses in the Delaware River. During time of war, the watertight mines were filled with explosives and placed in the river as a primary means of harbor defense. The mines were tethered by cables and could be electronically detonated from the shore. Fort Delaware appears in the above photograph on the left horizon. (Fort Delaware Society.)

Two

ENDICOTT ERA AND THE GREAT WORLD WAR
1893–1918

The mainland post entered a new phase at the turn of the century. In response to the Endicott Board recommendations, outdated guns were removed, and the post received its formal commission as Fort DuPont. The fort more than doubled its size with the acquisition of another 112 acres, and a major building campaign ensued. New buildings rapidly went up, including noncommissioned officers' quarters, barracks, a new guardhouse, a hospital, and a school. Concrete gun and mortar emplacements were completed between 1899 and 1904, and by 1915, the post had taken the shape of a traditionally laid out military reservation.

Just a few years later, a second rapid expansion took place. The remainder of the Reeves farm was bought, expanding the size of the post to its present appearance. The parade ground was the axis that separated enlisted men from officers and residential structures from utilitarian buildings. The road system became more complex, and wooden walkways were added next to many of them.

World War I transformed the post into a military site preparing for war. Newspaper accounts said that "Drafted Men Leave for Fort DuPont" for mobilization and basic training. In 1918, Mustard Pruett of the 7th Trench Mortar Battalion wrote, "I guess you will be surprised to know that I am ready to sail. Have everything but a cap, leggings, and a pick and shovel. Will get them in Fort DuPont." A new generation dawned for Fort DuPont as its role became that of quartermaster depot, training facility, and the command post for the Harbor Defenses of the Delaware. During World War I, the guns from Batteries Read, Gibson, and Ritchie were shipped elsewhere for use. After the war, Fort Saulsbury in Milford, Delaware, was complete and Fort DuPont was now in the secondary line of defense.

In June 1897, construction began on the mortar battery, originally planned to house sixteen 12-inch mortars equally distributed into four pits. The above photograph, facing eastward, shows the narrow gauge railroad expediting construction by delivering needed materials. This c. 1899 image was likely taken in the afternoon as evident by the shadow of the photographer with a dry plate camera. (Photograph by Frank C. Warner; Delaware Public Archives.)

Construction continues on the northeastern mortar pit in this 1898 photograph. The photographe[r] stood on the dirt-covered mine control casemate to capture this image. (Photograph by Frank C. Warner; Delaware Public Archives.)

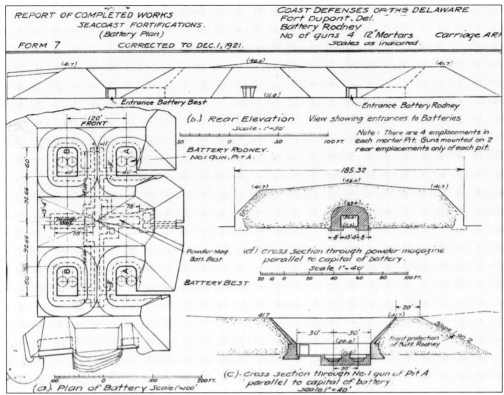

REPORT OF COMPLETED WORKS
SEACOAST FORTIFICATIONS.
(Battery Plan)
FORM 7   CORRECTED TO DEC. 1, 1921.

COAST DEFENSES OF THE DELAWARE
Fort Dupont, Del.
Battery Rodney
No of guns 4 12" Mortars   Carriage ARI
Scales as indicated.

The general plan shows the drainage pattern and internal layout of the mortar battery. Individual pits measured 40 feet by 60 feet. Construction costs amounted to about $217,721. The battery was configured as an "Abbot Quad" that was named after designer Brevet Brig. Gen. Henry L. Abbot. (National Archives.)

n February 17, 1898, workers are in initial stages of assembling the mortar platforms (Pit 1), which ll support the spring return carriages. The original post headquarters (built in 1898) appears in e background. (Photograph by Frank C. Warner; Delaware Public Archives.)

25

The cylinder brackets, recoil cylinder, trunnion cap square, and other carriage components appear newly assembled in this photograph, taken on February 17, 1898. Carriage 84 is in the foreground as noted by stenciled components. The carriages in the background are stenciled as (from left to right) 58, 56, and 83. (Photograph by Frank C. Warner; Delaware Public Archives.)

The M1890 M1 mortar rests on a M1896 M1 carriage while in the loading position. The gun h a range of about seven miles. (Photograph by Lamar Studio.)

The original headquarters (Building 23) is currently the oldest building on post. Built in 1898, the structure also served as officers' quarters, and later, housing for warrant officers. (National Archives.)

Before construction finished on the rifle battery, at least one 8-inch gun on a disappearing carriage was mounted. "There are sent you herewith the duplicate copy of Bill of Lading No. 62, dated April 13, 1898, and copy of the invoice of transfer, covering shipment of two 8-inch B.L. Rifles from Sandy Hook Proving Ground, to the U.S. Reservation near Delaware City. Upon receipt of the property please return the papers with the usual report. By direction of Major C.W. Raymond," is written by Stephen Lynch, chief clerk. (National Archives.)

This photograph was taken in 1899 from the parapet of the Twenty Gun Battery and shows the left flank of the nearly completed rifle battery. Construction started on May 1, 1898, and was completed by December 31, 1898. The rifle battery was the first Endicott-era emplacement completed on the reservation. (Photograph by Frank C. Warner; Delaware Public Archives.)

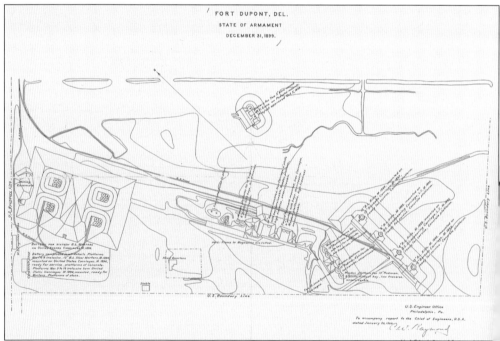

The rifle battery (right) was a split battery with 12-inch guns on either flank and 8-inch gun situated in the middle two emplacements. Remnants of Twenty Gun Battery also appear in th sketch. (Plan by Lt. Spencer Cosby; National Archives.)

Of the same series of photographs shown previously, this view shows the right flank of the emplacement. The coal-fired boiler can be seen through the open doors of the power station, and the already mounted eight-inch disappearing gun is also visible. (Delaware Public Archives.)

These modern batteries made use of the most up-to-date technologies available, including the wholesale use of electricity. Electricity illuminated the batteries, controlled the ammunition delivery systems, and the guns themselves were even electrically operated. Power for these systems was provided by a large coal-fired boiler, as seen above in the power station of the rifle battery. The boiler generated steam to power electrical dynamos. All of these power systems made use of direct current, as advocated by Thomas Edison. (Delaware Public Archives.)

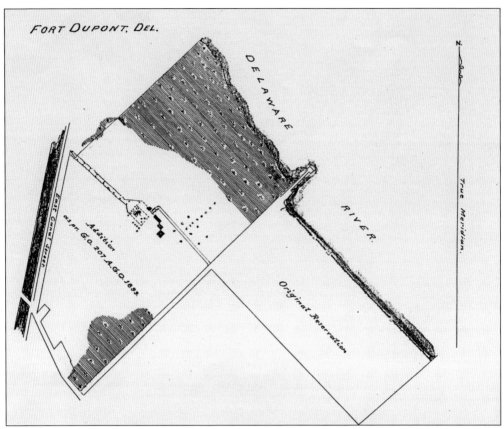

In 1899, James B. Henry sold 112 acres of his farm situated next to the original reservation acquired from Clement Reeves. During the Civil War, James Henry served as captain of Company H, 5th Delaware Infantry. Effective on July 22, 1899, "the battery at Delaware City" was named in honor of Rear Adm. Samuel Francis Du Pont. (National Archives.)

In July 1899, workers use a temporary ramp and pulley system to haul the 118-ton barbette carria[ge] into position. The M1892 carriage supported a 12-inch gun, M1888, which weighed 52 ton[s]. (Delaware Public Archives.)

On July 12, 1899, one of the 12-inch gun tubes is ready to be moved into place at the rifle battery. Standing alongside the tube is one of the African American laborers employed by the government at Fort DuPont. Countless African Americans were instrumental in the construction of the batteries at all three forts on the Delaware River. (Delaware Public Archives.)

From 1899 to 1900, officers' quarters (Building 22) were built next to headquarters, near the Twenty Gun Battery. Bonnie Bonner said of the quarters, "We had a rain barrel just behind the porch that collected rain water for washing hair, etc. We had awfully hard water on the post—I can remember my mother talking about the hardness and the problems that caused with laundry." (National Archives.)

On July 12, 1899, workers stand with a 12-inch gun tube nearly in place at the rifle battery's emplacement No. 1. The battery's two 12-inch guns were complemented with an additional six 12-inch guns equally distributed at Forts Delaware and Mott. (Delaware Public Archives.)

The sheer weight of the projectiles fired by these massive guns presented considerable problems in seemingly simple operations, such as moving rounds from the magazine to the gun deck. Engineers overcame these problems with the use of an overhead rail system and electrically operated hoists. This photograph, taken in 1900, shows the electric motor and controls for one of the Hodges back-delivery hoists in the rifle battery. Also note the overhead rail visible on the ceiling

Built in 1901, the post guardhouse (Building 16) is located directly west of the mortar battery. In one occurrence, two convicted deserters, along with another awaiting trial, escaped from the prison cells inside the guardhouse. According to the *Philadelphia Inquirer*, "The men had in some manner secured a jackknife, and with this cut through the floor. Then they dropped through a cellar way and walked out an open door. The police in all of the surrounding cities have been asked to look out for the men." (Delaware Historical Society.)

On February 14, 1902, the rifle battery was officially named in honor of George Read, signer of the Declaration of Independence. On July 25, 1902, Battery Read's guns were formally tested under the supervision of Col. Wallace Randolph. The *Philadelphia Inquirer* reported, "The guns were fired in turn until 13 shots had been fired from each of the 12-inch and 8-inch guns." What the article does not report is that a number of these projectiles skipped off the water and landed in New Jersey. Local residents refused to return two of the shells and proudly displayed them for decades at a local fire department in Salem, New Jersey. In this photograph, two unidentified girls stand next to one of those shells in 1908. In 2006, one of the shells was returned to Delaware and is now on display at Fort DuPont State Park. (Delaware State Parks.)

According to the Federal Writers' Project, "Soldiers from Fort Du Pont stroll with their town girls in grassy Battery Park [in Delaware City], where the whole community used to gather at evenings to see the *Lord Baltimore* or the *William Penn* enter the locks on the way from Philadelphia to Baltimore." On the left horizon, the houses along officers' row are visible. (Delaware Historical Society.)

This is one of the earliest known images of officers' row at Fort DuPont. The farmhouse of James B. Henry originally occupied the lot directly behind the photographer. This house was constructed around the time of the Chesapeake and Delaware Canal, and the road was the farmhouse's driveway. The fountain located in the foreground occupied the center of the estate original carriage turnaround. At the far end of officers' row was an entranceway, which feature two 24-pounder flank howitzers and stacks of cannonballs all from the Civil War era and like coming from Fort Delaware. According to official records, "There are 9 houses for officers quarter Three of these (Nos. 1, 8, 9) contain 9 rooms and bath each, and 6 houses (Nos. 2, 3, 4, 5, 6, contain 8 rooms and bath each." (Delaware Public Archives.)

An early 1900s, northeastern view shows Elm Avenue as a simple dirt road that is lined with young elm trees. The bachelor officer quarters (Building 44) appears on the left, followed by the post hospital, which is obscured from view. The new post headquarters (Building 10) is the two-story structure at the extreme end of the avenue. On the left horizon, quarters line along officers' row, which intersects with Elm Avenue in front of the post headquarters. Note the old farmhouse, which was originally located at the roundabout, has already been demolished. (Author's Collection.)

Two children watch the guard mount ceremony on the parade field closest to Elm Avenue. The flagstaff and post exchange and gymnasium building are visible in the background. In the distant right are wooden barracks (Building 13) and the slope (hill) of the mortar battery. Bonnie Bonner wrote, "Battery Hill was the sledding destination of every child on Fort du Pont. There were no worries about sliding into trees or into streets and traffic, so parents were not hesitant to let the kids (most all ages) go sledding without adult supervision. Skis were checked out from Quartermaster Supply when the snow crust was just right. It was only a short run down that hill, but it was still fun and seemed so sophisticated!" (Author's Collection.)

The post band is formed on the parade grounds, facing the colors, in this early 1900s postcard. The bachelor officer quarters (BOQ) appears in the background next to the hospital (Building 11). (Author's Collection.)

The BOQ (Building 44) served as housing for single officers, both permanent party and thos on temporary duty. (National Archives.)

RAPID FIRE GUN FT. DUPONT
LAMAR PHOTO

This 2.24-inch (six pounder) rapid-fire gun and its companion were located on either side of the flagstaff. The gun is a M1900 on a wheeled mount. In a time of war, this field piece (manufactured by Driggs-Seabury Co.) offered the mobility to defend the landward approach of Fort DuPont. A 1903 map detailing these defenses documents "field batteries and infantry redoubts," which extend as far south as St. Georges Creek and Port Penn, Delaware. The BOQ and hospital are visible in the distance. (Author's Collection.)

Gymnasium and Flag Staff - Fort Dupond, Delaware City, Del.

bove is an early view of the flagstaff located at the head of the parade field. In rear of the flagstaff the post exchange and gymnasium, which was built in 1906. The slope of the mortar batteries also visible at the far right. (Author's Collection.)

Another view of the rapid-fire guns next to the flagstaff plainly shows the post headquarters situated at the end of Elm Avenue in the background. Looking past the headquarters to the right are buildings in Delaware City. The trees in this image are maples, which line the length of Maple Boulevard. (Author's Collection.)

The post headquarters (Building 10), constructed in 1901, was the home to all administrativ functions at Fort DuPont. The first floor contained offices while the second floor had rooms fc courts-martial and records storage. (National Archives.)

Old 15 inch Guns and Gymnasium, Delaware City, Del.

The post exchange and gymnasium (Building 36) is situated at the head of the parade field directly behind the flagstaff. In the early 1900s, an unknown soldier at Fort DuPont wrote, "This building is a great deal larger than it looks, for they have bowling alleys, pool tables, restaurant, library, exchange, gym, balcony, dance hall, and all kinds of amusements there for the soldiers, but they pay for all they get there, except the exercise in the gym, and a fellow can get that at the YMCA on the outside of the post." (Delaware Historical Society.)

BARRACKS FT. DUPONT
LAMAR PHOTO

Outside the post exchange and gymnasium, looking down Maple Boulevard, soldiers stand by one of the 15-inch Rodman guns. The three wood-framed barracks line the right side of the road. Author's Collection.)

Company barracks (Buildings 13 and 14) along Maple Boulevard were the first constructed at Fort DuPont and followed standardized plans. These structures housed the Coast Artillery troops that garrisoned the post. Each barrack had latrines, showers, a library or reading room, two offices, a small squad room, kitchen, dining room, bread and china closet, two cook bedrooms, two large squad rooms, two small NCO rooms, and a barbershop. Directly behind the barrack buildings are two of the noncommissioned officer (NCO) quarters built in 1901. Senior NCOs occupied these duplexes (Buildings 15 and 16) with their families. (Delaware Historical Society.)

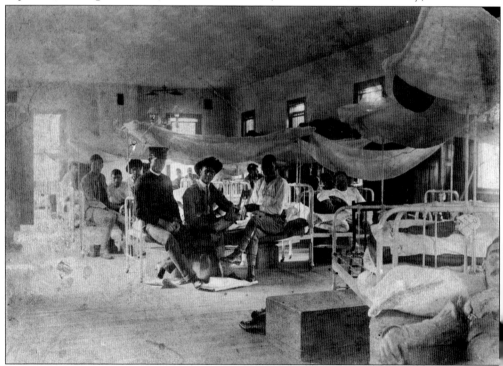

This photograph documents the living conditions of soldiers in the 112th Company, Coast Artillery Corps (CAC). Enlisted soldiers slept in open-bay rooms, such as this one, on cast-iron quartermaster beds. Note the mosquito netting hanging above the beds. The land on which Fort DuPont is situated is in the middle of large river marshes, the ideal breeding ground for mosquitoes. Nights spent in this area without the benefit of mosquito netting led to very little sleep. (William Mortimer Collection; Fort Delaware Society.)

This unknown soldier models the 1902–1905 dress uniform (minus the belt) with red breast cord complete with dual waffles. The soldier wears the M1902 service cap with crossed-cannon insignia and attached numerals that indicates he is a member of the 112th Company, CAC. Note the Army-issued blanket, which serves as a backdrop for this c. 1906 photograph. (William Mortimer Collection; Fort Delaware Society.)

"A happy bunch of the 112th" Company, CAC, shows off a variety of uniforms. Pvt. William Edward Mortimer (kneeling on the far left) is the original owner of this photograph. (Fort Delaware Society.)

This postcard shows one of the 12-inch rifled guns (M1888) on barbette carriages (M1892) mounted at Battery Read. Because of the need to hoist projectiles from the platform in order to load them, the rate of fire was considerably slower than that of the quicker disappearing guns. The M1888 had a range of about 8.5 miles, which was significantly less than later models manufactured in the 1890s. In July 1918, the two guns were moved to Fort Hamilton, New York. (Photograph by Lamar Studio.)

The 112th Company, CAC, pose outside the double-company barracks in this c. 1909 photograph. Note the sergeant seated on the extreme left with enough service stripes to be a veteran of the Indian Wars. Pvt. William Mortimer stands in the second row, sixth from the left. (Photograph by O.W. Waterman; Fort Delaware Society.)

"Night after the Ball" is handwritten on the reverse of this barrack photograph of the 112th Company, CAC. Men stationed at Fort DuPont would often hold social functions at their barracks. A 1908 article from the *Philadelphia Inquirer* describes such an event: "Lovers of dancing had a chance to revel in the pleasure of the waltz this week, and many took advantage of the opportunity offered by taking part in the big ball at the barracks of the Coast Artillery at Fort DuPont on Thursday night." (William Mortimer Collection; Fort Delaware Society.)

"To my friend Curly [Mortimer] from Vic" is written on the reverse of this cabinet card. The soldiers are, from left to right, (first row) Pvt. Victor Burgoh and Pvt. Glen Disby; (second row) Pvt. Clyde Ryan. All are from the 45th Company, CAC. (Fort Delaware Society.)

"Russel & Coddy" is handwritten on the back of this cabinet card photograph that once belonged to Pvt. William Mortimer of the 112th Company, CAC. The sitting soldier wears the insignia of a musician while the individual standing wears the crossed cannons of the artillery. This photograph dates from around 1906 or 1907. (Photograph by Wilmington Photo Company; Fort Delaware Society.)

A group of soldiers poses in the kitchen of the 112th Company, CAC, with assorted china, a cat, and a knife. Soldiers from each unit would be detailed to perform the cooking and washing duties for the rest of the men. Typically, cats were not part of the rations at Fort DuPont. (William Mortimer Collection; Fort Delaware Society.)

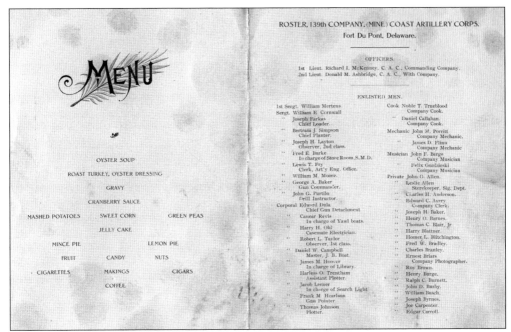

The 1909 Christmas menu for the 139th Company, (Mine) Coast Artillery Corps features oyster soup, turkey with oyster dressing, gravy, cranberry sauce, mashed potatoes, sweet corn, green peas, jelly cake, mince pie, lemon pie, fruit, candy, nuts, coffee, and makings, topped off with cigarettes and cigars. The unit cooks are listed as Noble T. Trueblood, Daniel Callahan, and John Ruzock. The menu further lists Elmer G. Renenbaugh as the assistant post baker. (William Mortimer Collection; Fort Delaware Society.)

The Christmas dinner, as described above, has been laid out in the mess hall located on the first floor of one of the barracks. The staff is lined up in front of the kitchen door, next to the small serving window. Cooks endeavored to prepare elaborate holiday meals such as this one to give soldiers a taste of home. Even fresh fruits and cigars are arranged on the tables as an extra treat. The image was likely taken by company photographer Pvt. Ernest Briars. (Fort Delaware Society.)

As the post expanded, more barracks buildings were needed to house the troops at Fort DuPont. In 1909, a double-company, brick barrack (Building 49) was built on Colver Road fronting on the parade ground, opposite of the BOQ and hospital. The band barracks (Building 48) was constructed to the right of the new barracks. During the same time, a one-story duplex to house firemen was also built on post. All were included in a $71,000 bid prepared by the Lynch Brothers, who were contractors. (Photograph by Nichols Studio.)

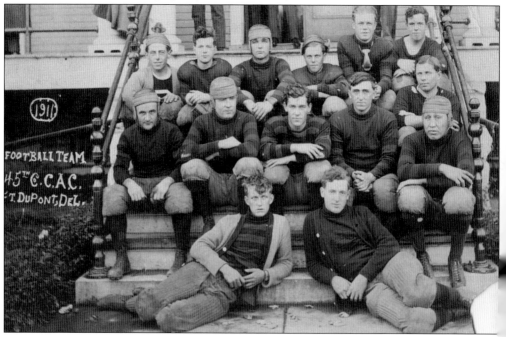

Pvt. William H. Press (front, left) and Pvt. Claude W. Jordan (back row, fourth from left) sit among soldiers from the 45th Company, CAC, outside of the wooden barracks (Building 42) closest to the guardhouse. Bill Press and Claude Jordan eventually married local girls and remained in Delaware City after discharge from the Army. Their military service helped both secure civilian jobs on post. During World War II, the post directory lists Jordan as chief plumber and Press as foreman for automobile mechanics in the motor pool. (Sally Jordan and Cynthia Jordan-Barber Collection.)

On July 7, year unknown, the mine planter *General E.O.S. Ord* was photographed off Fort DuPont while laying mines. This image was taken when the government was testing harbor mines. The *General Ord* was built in 1909 in Wilmington, Delaware. The ship served until 1946. (Photograph by International News Service.)

CONTACT MINES
READY TO BE LAID

Printed text on the reverse side of this image says, "Each one of these mines contains 100 pounds of gun cotton and when laid explodes immediately when anything comes in contact with it, like the keel or side of a ship. Here, you see a crew from the US mine planter, *General E.O.S. Ord*, after mine-planting practice off Fort DuPont. While not especially new, this type of marine mine has played an important part in the great European struggle and has sent many ships to the bottom. These mines are laid in the entrance of harbors to prevent the entrance of hostile ships." (Photograph by International Film Service, Inc.)

The baseball team of the 139th Company (Mine) was the Spaulding Trophy Champions in 1914. Above, a borrowed player (in the middle of the back row) joins the winning team outside the double-company barracks. (Photograph by Nichols Studio.)

Starting on August 1, 1911, following honorable discharge from the Army, Pvt. William Mortimer served as a civilian teamster for the 139th Company at Fort DuPont. He is seen (far left) holding the reigns of mule cart No. 1 of the Quartermaster Department. The building in the background is the post hospital. Note the post greenhouse in the distance on the far left. (Fort Delaware Society.)

In August 1915, the 112th Company, CAC, models newly obtained campaign hats with olive drab uniforms. The soldier sitting in the front, eighth from left, is Pvt. Eugene J. Germaine, the original owner of this photograph. (Photograph by J.J. Fisher; Delaware State Parks.)

Here is another view of soldiers from the 112th Company, CAC. This photograph was taken in 1915. (Francis Germaine Collection; Delaware State Parks.)

In the above postcard, c. 1913–1915, artillerists from the 112th Company, CAC, sit on what appears to be a 4.72-inch British Armstrong Gun on a wheeled mount. According to the *Philadelphia Inquirer*, "Booming of guns at Fort duPont at Delaware City today [November 10, 1913] gave rise to rumors that the troops had been ordered to prepare for war with Mexico and were brushing up on their shooting. The officers of the fort laughed at the idea and declared that the men were only engaging in field practice, which the regulations require from time to time. The style of practice was what caused many people to think of war, for the men of the Forty-fifth and One-hundred-and twelfth Companies were practicing with 4.7 inch howitzers mounted on wheels, which in case of war are taken to the front and used as siege guns. There was a target mounted on one end of Pea Patch Island, and the entire day eight guns were booming at this target, while small boats patrolled the river and kept boats out of the range of the guns. The men were using shells which exploded near or at the targets and were not using ordinary cannon balls." (Francis Germaine Collection; Delaware State Parks.)

A reporter stops to talk to soldiers from the 112th Company during field exercises sometime between 1913 and 1915. (Francis Germaine Collection; Delaware State Parks.)

At Nichols Studio in Delaware City, Corporal White and Corporal Hoover stand with Eugenia Thompson, Dagmar Thompson Hoover and son, and Elizabeth Thompson, as indicated by the handwriting on this real-photo postcard. Corporal White is likely Harry H. White of the 139th Company. Corporal Hoover is James M. Hoover of the 36th Company, CAC. Previously, he appears on the roster of the 139th Company and is listed as being "in charge of the library" on post. Dagmar Hoover is his wife. (Sally Jordan and Cynthia Jordan-Barber Collection.)

112th Company, CAC, soldiers pose for the camera while modeling their campaign hats in this real-photo postcard. (Francis Germaine Collection; Delaware State Parks.)

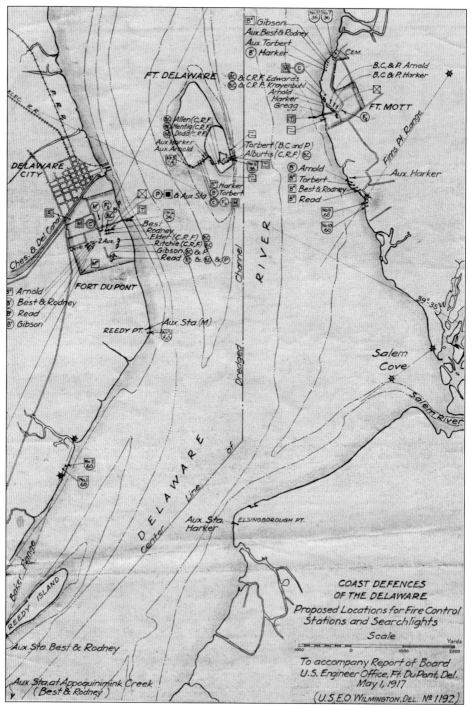

This Delaware River map, dated 1917, shows the locations of fire control stations and searchlights for Forts DuPont, Delaware, and Mott. The three forts made use of a network of centralized fire control to aim their guns. Rather than working as individual posts, the three forts worked closely to provide accurate firing data for all the guns. (National Archives, Philadelphia Branch.)

On March 8, 1918, "Battery A" forms outside the double-company barracks at Fort DuPont. The post commanders house (Building 50) appears on the left, followed by the headquarters building, service club (Building 126), and post exchange. This unit is likely Battery A, 7th Trench Mortar Battalion (Bn.), which according to official records, was stationed at the fort when this photograph was taken. "I am glad we are on our way, for when a man is [here] he is pretending to do his bit, but when he is over there he will do it, of course. Some of us may fall down on examination, but I do hope I won't. Tell everybody I am happy, and also tell the girls to stay single until we get back from Berlin," wrote Mustard Pruett, Battery D, 7th Trench Mortar Bn. The unit left for France on October 31, 1918. (James Thompson Collection; Fort Delaware Society.)

Individual cooking done by "Battery A" takes place in the horse paddock area in March 1918. The quartermaster stables (Building 17) are visible past the smoke on the extreme left. The backside of the quartermaster storehouse (Building 43) appears on the distant right. (James Thompson Collection; Fort Delaware Society.)

In this c. 1918 photograph, Pvt. James Davis, dressed in his denim coveralls, stands by the muzzle of a 12-inch mortar at Fort DuPont. Note the station in the rear used to transmit firing data from the plotting room to the gunners below. (Photograph by Nichols Studio; Delaware State Parks.)

This photograph shows a 12-inch mortar (M1890 M1) in firing position at Fort DuPont. Following construction of the mortar battery, it was eventually divided into two batteries: Caesar Rodney and Clermont Best. Battery Rodney was named after the signer of the Declaration of Independence on February 14, 1902. Battery Best was named on January 25, 1906, in honor of Maj. Clermont Best, who was an officer during the Spanish-American War. (Photograph by Lamar Studio; Delaware State Parks.)

Pvt. James Davis sits on the carriage of a 12-inch mortar at Fort DuPont around 1918. On October 21, 1918, according to the *Philadelphia Inquirer*, "One hundred drafted men left this city [Wilmington, Delaware] this afternoon for Fort duPont, where they will be trained for the Army. The men were accompanied to the station by a band, but on account of the epidemic of influenza the ceremonies were not so elaborate as usual." In the years following this photograph and according to Neil Lewis, "My brother and sister used to climb all over the guns, including the breeches. I was afraid to. The breech blocks had been removed for some purposes and the bores were quite clean and oily. Bunkers were located immediately behind each gun, presumably to hold the ammo. They had large steel doors that were very securely locked. As kids, we tried to get into everything!" (Photograph by Nichols Studio; Delaware State Parks.)

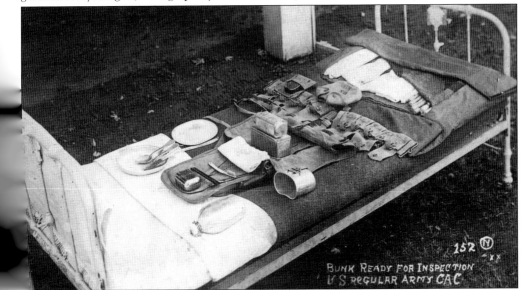

An image from the collection of Pvt. James Davis provides a detailed layout of the personal equipment of a soldier during the Great World War. (Photograph by Nichols Studio; Delaware State Parks.)

The post band plays on the northern end of the parade field in this c. 1918 photograph. The original framed barracks appear on the far left, and the double-company barracks appear in the center. According to Neil Lewis, "The parade ground seemed large to me. A REAL bugler played taps at sundown and the small howitzer was fired. My Dad had enough seniority in rank that he did not have to pull the taps-playing duty. He played trumpet and cornet." (Delaware Historical Society.)

An undated photograph, likely taken in the late 1910s, shows the Fort DuPont band at the "Shaw Co. Flag Raising." The Army band is wearing the summer version of the service uniform. (Delaware Military Heritage and Education Foundation.)

On the back of this real-photo postcard, Cpl. John E. Dunn, Headquarters Company, wrote, "Dear Friend, suppose you are shooting some game, [but I] wish I could hunt a few days. I like the Army life good. I was signed (corporal) this week, [but] I only regret I couldn't have gone across." (Photograph by Nichols Studio; Fort Delaware Society.)

Pvt. Carl Peterson, with blue eyes and sandy-colored hair, enlisted in the Pennsylvania Army National Guard in 1914. A year later, he signed up for active duty, eventually deploying to Panama during World War I. During his military career, he also ended up at Fort DuPont. After his discharge in 1920, he joined the Chester Police Department eventually retiring as head of the vice squad in 1944. During World War II, he was denied entry in both the US and Canadian armies due to his age. In 1945, Carl was awarded the FBI Medal of Honor for exposing a Japanese sabotage operation while executing his normal police duties. In 1965, his son Edward F. "Pete" Peterson founded the Delaware City Marina, across the branch canal from Fort DuPont. According to Pat Peterson, "I pumped gas on the original dock, which still stands with the gas pump on it, during the summer of 1965. There was no building behind the dock at that time, so it was very lonely work for me as a teenager. My grandfather, Carl Peterson, would ride down from Chester several times a week to keep me company on the open dock. It was during these visits that I learned about Fort DuPont for the first time and he would tell me stories about the days when he was stationed there. I only wish that I had had the wisdom at that time to write those stories down. My grandfather was small in stature but a giant among men and he taught us by his example the importance of making our world a safer place for everyone." (P. Patricia Peterson Collection.)

This c. 1918 image shows the football yards and baseball green on the parade field at Fort DuPont. This image was likely taken from a third-story dormer or window in the double-company barracks. (Photograph by Nichols Studio; Delaware State Parks.)

As Fort DuPont expanded, more room was needed at the post hospital. In response, a secor floor was added to the right wing of the hospital building. Photographic evidence suggests th happened around 1912. (National Archives.)

Three

BETWEEN THE WARS
1919–1938

While the time between World War I and World War II saw a decrease in active military preparation, Fort DuPont still played a critical role in coastal defense. The new age of air warfare changed the face of coastal artillery, as defenses of the Delaware River and Bay were moving south with greater range of fire. The only remaining armament at Fort DuPont consisted of eight mortars and the three-inch guns of Battery Elder. The primary defense on the Delaware River now consisted of two pairs of 12-inch guns on long-range carriages at Fort Saulsbury in Milford. Fort DuPont's role was that of a secondary line of defense.

The post took shape as a location for training Army engineers. The 1st Engineer Regiment arrived in 1922, and by the mid-1930s, it was led by Col. Ulysses S. Grant III. Training included reserve engineer units as well as the Citizens Military Training Camps. The community buzzed with activity despite the Depression. Officers' houses weighing as much as 240 tons were floated over from Fort Mott via pontoon and a war department theater was constructed. The Civilian Conservation Corps and the Works Progress Administration were put to work performing improvements at the fort, including laying sewer lines, digging wells, and the construction of four brick senior NCO duplexes (with the aid of the First Engineers).

Neil Lewis, son of S.Sgt. Fay G. Lewis, recalled Depression times at the post growing up. Not able to visit the cinema often due to the cost, he and his siblings were regularly sent to the commissary to purchase day-old bread for 2¢. This was a significant saving of 1¢ for the freshly baked bread. His memories include going barefoot in the summer, flying kites at the post golf course, football games on the parade ground, and clambering over coast artillery guns. Another kid, John "Sonny" Bonner, had a not-so-memorable moment when playing on top of Batteries Read and Gibson fell from a catwalk, sustained a broken leg, and spent several weeks recovering at Walter Reed General Hospital.

This 1927 bird's-eye view shows the hedge line of the original reservation. The two rapid-fire batteries (foreground) are John Ritchie and Samuel Elder (right). Battery Ritchie was named honor of the artillery captain killed at Lundy's Lane during the War of 1812. This emplaceme supported two 5-inch guns and was built in 1900. These M1900 guns, mounted on M1903 pedesta were removed in May 1917. (Photograph by 14th Photograph Section; National Archives.)

MAR 1926

This photograph, taken in 1926, shows the wharf (Building 37) at Fort DuPont. Note the narro gauge railroad running the length of the dock, along with the covered storage building temporarily hold shipments until they could be transported to their destinations. During th 1920s, Fort DuPont's artillery troops were scaled down, and the 1st Engineer Regiment made th fort their new duty station. (National Archives.)

240-TON HOUSE MOVED ACROSS RIVER

This substantial 16-room house, weighing 240 tons, was on its way to its new foundations at Fort Du Pont, ving been moved across the Delaware River from Fort Mott, N. J., yesterday. Photo shows the tug Sylvester ving the dwelling into the mouth of the old Chesapea ke and Delaware Canal. Three other buildings are t) moved this week for the purpose of solving an acute housing problem at Fort Du Pont.

e population at Fort DuPont continued to rise in the 1920s and more housing was needed. At same time, Fort Mott in New Jersey was only kept on caretaker status. Because of this, the :ision was made to move a number of officers' quarters from Mott to DuPont. In December 31, the first house (Building 81) was moved as practice before endeavoring to relocate several ner quarters. According to the *Philadelphia Inquirer*, the "four-and-half mile journey required hour and 48 minutes and was completed as darkness fell." The exercise was conducted by the Engineer Regiment. (Fort Delaware Society.)

year later, on
·cember 12, 1932,
 more quarters
·re similarly floated
·oss on barges.
·e double officers'
·arters in this
·age (Building
· was one of the
·ildings originally
·cted at Fort Mott.
·ational Archives.)

Located on Staff Lane, the quartermaster office (Building 113) was one of the busiest hubs on the post. The quartermaster department handled everything from supply requisitions and building management to troop transportation. (National Archives.)

Warrant Officer Edward A. Bonner holds his daughter Veronica "Bonnie" Bonner in this snapshot taken in Panama during 1927. Bonner, a veteran of the Great World War, served as quartermaster at Fort DuPont from 1928 until 1941. According to Bonnie, "While at Fort DuPont, he was known as the 'go to guy!' If you wanted something accomplished or needed an answer to a vexing problem, he was the person people turned to repeatedly. He was instrumental in garnering interest in the local American Legion (Delaware City, Robert L. Taylor Post No. 13). He enabled that organization to gain permission to hold their monthly meetings in the service hut on post and did likewise for the ladies of the American Legion Auxiliary. [My dad] served many terms as the legion post commander and [my mother] likewise as president of the auxiliary. Both placed high emphasis on their respective organizations reaching out to help those in need." Bonner was commissioned a major in January 1941 and assigned to the Quartermaster School in Philadelphia as an instructor. In 1944, he retired as a lieutenant colonel after 44 years of military service. (Photograph by Violet Bonner.)

Margaret Violet Bonner, with daughters Veronica ("Bonnie") and Genevieve ("Gene," standing), appear in this photograph taken in 1927 while living in the Panama Canal Zone. An accomplished dressmaker, Violet designed and sewed many of the clothes for her daughters and herself. Sewing curtains, throws, pillows, and more added flair to their quarters and soon had other Army wives asking her to help decorate their bleak quarters. Shortly after their arrival at Fort DuPont in 1928, the family was blessed with the addition of a son, John Edward Bonner. Bonnie Bonner noted, "Here we lived in Quarters 22 situated along Maple Boulevard, and my mother put her sewing skills to work in transforming the drab interior (all walls were painted "Army buff") to a pleasing, colorful palette. My mother also became associated with church, school, and civic organizations, often serving as the president. Through her efforts the American Legion Auxiliary visited monthly, Perry Point Veteran Hospital (Perryville, Maryland), organizing card and board games for the residents, serving refreshments, and occasionally providing musical programs. Sewing outfits for the annual Christmas plays and creating Halloween costumes were just two of my mother's many service projects for the military families at Fort DuPont." (Bonnie Rorabaugh Collection.)

n 1930, Gene and Bonnie Bonner appear with tricycles outside the topographical shop (Building 0) near their home on Maple Boulevard. Besides riding, kids on post enjoyed the post exchange's oda fountain and ice cream parlor, swimming pool, movie theater, and the annual Christmas lay organized by Chaplain Westcott. (Photograph by Violet Bonner.)

The War Department Theatre (Building 29) was the feature attraction at Fort DuPont in 1933. The First Engineers and Works Progress Administration (WPA) built the 398-seat theater situated next to the post headquarters. Dual carbon-arc projectors (to facilitate quick reel changes) illuminated the silver screen during the Depression era. The cheap ticket price and escape from reality made this one of the most popular places on post. (Photograph by Pvt. William M. Thomas.)

Capt. Edgar P. Reese never used this book of "Fort DuPont Theatre Tickets" issued to him while at the fort. The tickets guaranteed discounted admission for Army personnel. Delaware City civilians, without these, would pay full price for admission. (Fort Delaware Society.)

Pvt. Francis H. Walshe of Company A, 1st Engineer Regiment, was born in Liverpool, England, and according to Army records had "blue eyes, brown hair, ruddy complexion, and was 5 feet 8 1/2 inches in height." While stationed at Fort DuPont, he earned his plasterers certification, which cited his "performance of school duty [was] very satisfactory, qualified [as] assistant instructor." (Katherine Walshe Collection; Delaware State Parks.)

Besides the theater, the engineers built four identical NCO duplexes in 1933. The above photograph features the duplex (Building 91) that faces Staff Lane. In the background, another duplex (Building 92) faces the other direction and shows the rear profile. (National Archives.)

Soldiers from the 1st Engineer Regiment, gather outside their barracks (Building 13 or 14) in this photograph taken around 1934 or 1936. These barracks were located on Maple Boulevard, just down the street from the post exchange. (Photograph by Pvt. William M. Thomas.)

Pvt. William Thomas stands with arms crossed in civilian attire for this 1936 photograph. The soldier standing at ease is identified as First Sergeant Lavigne of Company D. The guardhouse is visible in the background behind the stationary automobile. Although facing away from the camera, "no parking" graces the lower right sign. (Barry Thomas Collection.)

An unknown soldier with a dog appears outside the guardhouse in this 1930s snapshot. Note the fire ladders hung along the porch. Although not their intended purpose, residents often used these ladders to change out window screens between seasons. On the right, Private Thomas, with rifle and bayonet, strikes a pose outside the post guardhouse. (Barry Thomas Collection.)

Pvt. William Thomas stands with his girl while dressed in his Class A uniform. This snapshot was likely taken in Delaware City (or elsewhere) as the building architecture does not match any structures at Fort DuPont. Soldiers often spent free time in town and had their share of local girlfriends. Private Thomas, born in Milford, Delaware, enlisted at Fort DuPont in November 1933 at the age of 8. While at the fort, he was a member of Company D of the 1st Engineer Regiment. (Barry Thomas Collection.)

A 1934 snapshot shows the gasoline filling station (Building 79) located behind the post commissary (grocery store) on Service Road. (National Archives.)

An unidentified soldier stands by a 1930 to 1931 Ford Model A, likely a sport coupe or cabriolet. (Photograph by Pvt. William M. Thomas.)

Pvt. William Thomas stands on the left in both of these snapshots taken inside the barracks. The other soldiers are unidentified. (Barry Thomas Collection.)

n this photograph, taken around 1934, a soldier demonstrates inspection arms inside his barracks. 3arry Thomas Collection.)

It was not all fun and games for soldiers at Fort DuPont. The rifle range was used to keep soldiers proficient in the use of small arms. The range was located south of Batteries Read and Gibson. The soldiers in the photograph are likely from Company A or D of the 1st Engineer Regiment. (Delaware State Parks.)

These unidentified soldiers are from Company A, 1st Engineer Regiment. Note the unit's distinctive insignia visible on the left campaign hat. (Delaware State Parks.)

An unidentified soldier is shown in light marching order complete with a M1903 Springfield Rifle. On the right, Pvt. William Thomas stands by (what looks like) a 1934 Diamond T pickup truck. (Barry Thomas Collection.)

In this photograph, taken around 1934 or 1936, several dozen soldiers march outside barracks along Maple Boulevard. Photograph by Pvt. William M. Thomas.)

A desperate moment in time is preserved in this snapshot taken in February 1936. The post fire department attempts to extinguish flames emanating in the double-company barracks of the First Engineers. Pvt. William Thomas, a "chauffeur" by military occupation, often drove the post fire truck. (Photograph by Pvt. William M. Thomas.)

A local newspaper reported, "Uncle Sam sustained a loss estimated at $100,000 when barracks housing two companies of the First Engineers, US Army, were destroyed by fire at Fort DuPont early Friday morning. In addition to the fire department of the fort, are companies from Delaware City, Odessa, Middletown and New Castle fought the blaze and kept the flames from spreading to other buildings." The local newspaper article also reported the structure was barracks for Company C and the HQ Company. (Photograph by Pvt. William M. Thomas.)

According to the newspaper article, "Rural firemen on arriving found that it would be impossible to save the barracks where the fire started and spent much of their time in keeping the flames from spreading to the band barracks, about 20 feet away, and other close structures. The band barracks was soaked with water to keep the sparks from getting it afire. When the fire was under control only the walls of part of the barracks were left standing. The roof had caved in and also portions of the walls." (Photograph by Pvt. William M. Thomas.)

The barrack remnants are visible in this bird's-eye view taken on May 1, 1936. Note the football and baseball fields on the parade ground. (National Archives.)

Pvt. William Thomas (left) stands with another soldier outside the firehouse, which is located next to the barracks of Company D. The fire truck is probably a liberty truck (or some type of conversion), which had a top speed of about 15 miles per hour. (Barry Thomas Collection.)

Soldiers accused of misconduct were not the only individuals held in the guardhouse. The young son of Warrant Officer Bonner spent an afternoon behind bars due to one of his legendary escapades. Neil Lewis remembered, "On one occasion, a motorized piece of equipment was left on the parade ground [. . .] An acquaintance kid of ours managed to get it started and it started chug-chug-chugging across the parade ground at a very slow pace. The entire fort erupted into a Keystone Kops scenario with everyone running about trying to figure out how to stop the juggernaut!" Bonnie Bonner said, "Here we go with the tale of my naughty little brother. The various escapades of little Sonny (John) Bonner were legend [at the fort]. But his joy ride in the old steam roller on the parade ground topped them all. Only a quick acting Army sergeant saved the day that time. But our father had had enough! 'Put him in the guard house,' he instructed the sergeant. 'Maybe it will teach him a lesson.' A couple of hours later when my father and I showed up at the guardhouse to gain Sonny's release, we found a tearful-eyed little fellow. Hugs and kisses and promises to never do that again brought about a happy ending." (Photograph by Pvt. William M. Thomas.)

Pvt. William M. Thomas looks out the driver-side window of an early model (1932–1934 range) Dodge pickup truck. Private Thomas was stationed at Fort DuPont from November 1933 until October 1936. (Barry Thomas Collection.)

First Engineer soldiers appear with one of their trucks in this mid-1930s photograph. During this period, the unit was commanded by Col. Ulysses S. Grant III. According to a local newspaper, "Having completed two years duty as post commander at Fort DuPont, Colonel Grant has been expecting a transfer. He will be on duty at Governors Island for two years." The article further mentions, "Colonel Grant is the grandson of Gen. Ulysses S. Grant, Civil War general and former president of the United States." (Delaware State Parks.)

The 1936 view from the water tower, facing southeast, shows a few temporary buildings and a coast artillery tower which, at one time, functioned as the primary station for Batteries Best, Rodney, and Read. The tower also served as a secondary station for Battery Arnold (at Fort Mott) and Battery Gibson. Twenty Gun Battery, complete with wooden stairs, is visible along the far left tree line. To the right are Batteries Read and Gibson. (Katherine Walshe Collection; Delaware State Parks.)

Pvt. William M. Thomas (left) and an unknown officer sit at the base of the coast artillery tower located at the intersection of Staff and Battery Lanes. This structure once served as the groupment command post and meteorological station. On October 31, 1936, Private Thomas was honorably discharged from the Army. He married his girlfriend, Hazel M. Draper, about two weeks before his discharge at Fort DuPont. Together, they eventually had three sons, the youngest being Barry Thomas. During World War II, William Thomas served as a city police officer in Wilmington, Delaware, until he was injured while on duty. In 1980, he retired after years as an inspector for the Delaware DMV. (Barry Thomas Collection.)

Front left to right, Gene, Bonnie, and Sonny Bonner appear outside their quarters in 1937. According to Bonnie, "We were known as the Bonner trio whenever we all went together someplace. We'd take bike hikes (that's what we called them) over to Delaware City—sometimes adding a bike rider or two as we went, till we ended up at the soda shop (Heal's newsstand with soda fountain store) to get a phosphate (orange or lemon or lime) price of 5¢ for the big glass!" The guardhouse, engineer buildings, and topographical shop all appear in the background. A portion of the mortar battery is visible, distant right. (Photograph by Violet Bonner.)

The Bonner home (Building 22), complete with green-, orange-, and white-striped window treatments appear in this image, dated around 1936. The first floor contains the master bedroom (first window), bathroom (half window), girl's room (third and fourth windows), kitchen (fifth and sixth windows), and entryway (seventh window). The other side of the house has a dining room and living area. Stairs from the kitchen lead to the finished attic, which contained Sonny's bedroom. (Photograph by Violet Bonner.)

In a late 1930s snapshot, Sergeant Lavigne and Senator appear with Sonny and Bonnie Bonner during trick-riding lessons in the paddock area. The red-and-white checkered water tower, located near Reeves Lane, is visible in the background. (Photograph by Edward Bonner.)

Bonnie Bonner, Sergeant Lavigne, and Senator clear a hurdle during a halftime show on the football field at Fort DuPont. Bonnie said of the moment, "My cowgirl hat was blown off my head and only the little strap kept it on me." (Photograph by Violet Bonner.)

Four

WORLD WAR II

As the 1930s drew to a close, life seemed uneventful at Fort DuPont. Doug Shreve, son of Lt. Col. Arthur L. Shreve, recalled the benefits of being the son of a high-ranking officer. Ironically, Doug's great-grandfather Thomas Jefferson Shreve had been a Civil War prisoner at Fort Delaware. Wearing an officer's cap from the post tailor shop, the boy enjoyed doughnuts from the post bakery, pausing at the flagpole in the evening as colors were lowered. His uncle Bill, also posted to Fort DuPont, described sleepy Delaware City as "the only graveyard he had ever seen with a traffic signal in the middle of it."

Then, a December day in 1941 changed life overnight. The post football team was playing against a team from Milleville, New Jersey, when news came of Pearl Harbor. The devastating news put all posts on alert, and the security of the Delaware River and Bay took on renewed importance. By 1943, Forts DuPont, Delaware, and Mott were formally eliminated from the harbor defenses, with that role now going to Fort Miles in southern Delaware. Fort DuPont's role changed not only physically, but also in purpose. Large numbers of temporary or mobilization buildings were quickly erected. Fort DuPont was now a key training post for skills including combat, communication, chemical warfare, and even baking.

The post also assumed a new role as a prisoner of war camp. Nearly 3,000 captured Germans from Rommel's Afrika Korps, along with soldiers from the European theatre, were imprisoned in repurposed buildings while they assisted the American war effort in the farm fields and on the post. Kurt Henkel, one of the German prisoners, said in a 2007 letter, "I like to remember those days since I was treated well. I was lucky to be taken a US prisoner of war and have thus been able to survive the war." Colonel Shreve, once deputy commander at Fort DuPont, was not so fortunate. Sent to war in the Philippines, he survived the Bataan Death March and four years as a Japanese prisoner of war.

This bird's-eye view, dated 1927, shows the rapid-fire batteries with newly planted trees in rear for concealment. Battery Elder (on the right) was the last battery staffed at Fort DuPont. After the attack on Pearl Harbor, Elder was manned 24 hours a day. Her three-inch guns remained in place until 1942, when they were sent to a temporary emplacement, known as Elder II, situated just south of Reedy Island next to the Liston Range Lighthouse. Ritchie's guns were removed much earlier, hence the unkempt appearance. The waterproof tar coating is cracked and in disrepair. (National Archives, Philadelphia Branch.)

On September 26, 1939, Lt. Col. Joseph C. Mehaffey, post commander, documented the condition of Battery Ritchie in a letter to his superior. He said, "This battery was constructed in 1900, received its armament of two 5-inch guns in 1906, and was dismantled in 1917. It is not a part of any defense project, nor is it of any future military or historical value. No work has been done on the care and preservation of the emplacement since the armament was removed, and it is in such a state of deterioration as to be an eyesore, and unfit for any possible use. Five small photographs of the emplacement are enclosed herewith." (National Archives, Philadelphia Branch.)

Col. R.T. Ward, Chief of Engineers, Second Corps Area, responded with a "Dear Mehaffey" letter on October 3, 1939. He said, "We consider the old batteries at Fort DuPont to be of historic value, and [. . .] they added to the picturesque quality of the post. The policy is to leave the batteries and not tear them up in order to get a small amount of material for WPA work." (National Archives.)

On October 5, 1939, Colonel Mehaffey offered his rebuttal by official correspondence. "I am more interested than the average officer in historical relics, and I am certainly interested in the appearance of Fort DuPont. What we want from Ritchie is primarily the old concrete, [and] without the improvement of the road system, this post will soon be brought to a stop." Mehaffey's request was eventually granted and demolition took place in 1940. (National Archives.)

With America's involvement in World War II on the horizon, dozens of temporary buildings were constructed on the post in 1940. The work was completed by contractors, engineers, and remaining WPA workers. A photograph taken from the water tower shows the hospital complex (back left) and cantonment barracks (right). These two-story barracks housed soldiers and were later used to hold German prisoners of war. (National Archives.)

In 1940, the Headquarters Battery, 21st Coast Artillery, stands in company formation outside their newly built barracks (Building 24) on Colver Road. According to the *Coastal Bursts*, the unit was established following the inactivation of Battery E, 7th Coast Artillery, at Fort DuPont. (Fort Delaware Society.)

The *Coastal Bursts* reports, "Administration, communication, and transportation, and other functions of such a unit, have been provided capably by the personnel of Headquarters Battery since its activation on February 1, 1940. The personnel have changed considerably from the original roster of 41 enlisted men and one officer, but we . . . maintain that quality of service is unchanged." (Fort Delaware Society.)

On October 19, 1940, Col. J.C. Mehaffey reported that the "present garrison comprises, in addition to the usual service detachments, Company A, 30th Engineer Battalion (top), 115 men; the 1st Engineer Battalion, now recruiting to 628 men; the 70th Engineer Company (L. Pon.), 165 men; and Regimental Headquarters and Battery A, 21st Coast Artillery, 129 men." The above band, likely that of the 21st Coast Artillery, appears sometime in 1941. (Fort Delaware Society.)

The Chapel (Building E-215) was one of the temporary buildings constructed and dedicated on Sunday, October 12, 1941. (Delaware Public Archives.)

According to Lt. Lemiah G. Butt, post chaplain, "The first object which attracts the eye of the individual as he enters the chapel is the altar." Behind the altar is a triptych painted by artist Nina Barr Wheeler and dedicated to St. Barbara, the patron saint of artillery. On August 9, 1942, it was presented by "Mrs. Junius Morgan, Chairman of the Citizens Committee for the Army and Navy Inc." Above is the altar configuration for Roman Catholic mass. The *Fort DuPont Flashes* reported that Protestant and Jewish services were also offered on post. (Photograph by F.A. Burnett.)

Col. George Ruhlen (right) commanded Fort DuPont from November 4, 1940, until late 1944. He was a longtime coast artillery veteran whose previous assignments included Fort Mills in the Philippines. On December 20, 1940, Colonel Ruhlen wrote, "Unofficial information indicates that the contractor will not complete the buildings for the 21st CA until January 10th. I'll confirm this officially by January 2nd. Major Butler, 1st Engr. Bn. [Engineer Battalion], states his organization is due at Fort Devens, January 17th." Colonel Ruhlen was an avid historian, who amassed a rather large collection of Fort DuPont photographs and related correspondence. In the 1960s and 1970s, he donated most of his collection to the Fort Delaware Society, including this image. (Fort Delaware Society.)

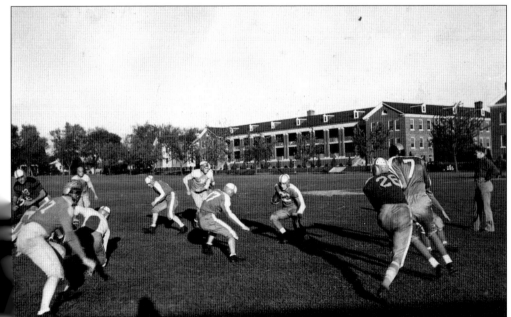

The parade ground, originally intended for drill and parades, multipurposed as a bustling sports complex. A baseball diamond and football field, complete with bleachers, was erected for the popular past times. In the image above, the football team practices with the newly rebuilt double company barracks. (Fort Delaware Society.)

On the left, Lt. Levin Gale "Bill" Shreve and older brother Lt. Col. Arthur L. Shreve Jr. stand outside of their quarters (Building 6) in spring 1941. Colonel Shreve served as post quartermaster and deputy post commander from 1940 to 1941. According to Doug Shreve, "As post quartermaster, Dad had a box built in the movie theater so Col. and Mrs. Ruhlen wouldn't have to fight to get a seat at the movies. I understand from what was said for years around my house that Mrs. Ruhlen was a little witchy . . . that was proven when I received my first bicycle for Christmas in 1940 . . . [when I] promptly learned to balance and ride the thing, but hadn't mastered the brakes . . . [I] went down the curb, across the circle (or semi-circle), and through the Ruhlen's hedge. My parents had to deal with the ire of Mrs. Ruhlen." (Doug Shreve Collection.)

Doug Shreve (left) said farewell to his father, Col. Arthur L. Shreve, on October 7, 1941. Colonel Shreve was transferred to General MacArthur's staff on the Philippine Islands. According to a news clipping, "Col. Arthur L. Shreve of Baltimore, who was reported missing in action following the fighting on Bataan and Corregidor, is a prisoner of the Japanese in an unidentified prison camp in the Philippines." In 1945, it was reported that Colonel Shreve survived the Bataan Death March and four years as a prisoner of war. Interestingly, Bill and Arthur's grandfather was a Confederate prisoner held at Fort Delaware during the Civil War. According to Doug, "my portrait was taken in the Spring of 1942 when I was still the same age as my last few months at DuPont." (Doug Shreve Collection.)

"Mom and Agnes" attended visitors' day in 1941. Bonnie Bonner stated, "In those days, young ladies did not visit military installations without being accompanied by mothers or aunts. The wearing of hats to all events was absolutely customary for all generations, but not so the length of one's dress. The younger ones could wear the shorter skirts and still be considered properly attired, whereas the greater the generational gap, the longer the dress would have to be." A newly built wooden barracks completes the backdrop of this snapshot. "Typical of the buildings being constructed at Fort DuPont is this barrack. It will be well-insulated, have a double floor, and will be heated by a hot-air forced circulation system," according to the *Journal-Every Evening* on December 3, 1940. (Delaware Historical Society.)

Members of the 122nd Coast Artillery Battalion (Antiaircraft) of the New Jersey Army National Guard conduct a driver training course outside their barracks. These were some of the temporary buildings constructed during 1940 to facilitate the influx of troops. The various buildings were built by the Belgrade and Hadley Construction Companies and the WPA. (Fort Delaware Society.)

Pvt. Ralph J. Santeramo (center) of the 122nd Coast Artillery wrote, "It took about a week to get settled. We got our new uniforms and other equipment, plus KP and Guard Duty. Also, [we received] our rifles, old 1903-bolt action. [We did] lots of drilling, long marching, and [made] jelly sandwiches for when we go on these marches. We had to get six weeks' infantry training, and we were restricted and could not get any passes yet." (Delaware State Parks.)

"Battery A was a Searchlight and Gun Control Group. Batteries B, C, and D were Antiaircraft Guns four large guns in each Battery," according to Pvt. (later Sgt.) Ralph Santeramo, standing left. His unit arrived at the fort on February 3, 1941, for a year's mobilization. (Delaware State Parks.)

"The days went by fast, what with all the training and getting our searchlights to keep us even more busy. We would go down the river and fire the large guns at targets that were towed by airplanes. Around midsummer we got rid of our searchlights and got the radar equipment. At that time I was made a sergeant of the Radar Section," as stated by Ralph Santeramo, who is standing on the left of this photograph taken in May 1941. (Delaware State Parks.)

On December 7, 1941, Ralph Santeramo was home in Jersey City, New Jersey, on a 24-hour pass and was "listening to the radio when an emergency announcement flashed a bulletin that all military personnel were to report back to their outfits as soon as possible." On December , following the attack on Pearl Harbor, the 122nd Coast Artillery left for duty on the West Coast. (Delaware State Parks.)

In February 1941, the 261st Coast Artillery, Delaware Army National Guard, arrived at Fort DuPont. These troops were assigned to man the remaining batteries at Fort DuPont and Fort Delaware. This image shows members of the 261st in line at the train station in Delaware City. The station no longer exists, but it was originally located near the corner of William and Monroe Streets. (Delaware Military Heritage and Education Foundation.)

Cpl. William A. Smith (left) and Sgt. Phil Moore appear in this 1941 snapshot. Note the experimental version of the field jacket worn by Corporal Smith. Both soldiers are members of Battery C, 261st Coast Artillery Battalion. During the war, Smith volunteered for paratrooper duty, which resulted in his service in the European Theatre. In 1945, he returned home after being awarded the Bronze Star and Combat Infantry Badge. After the war, Smith was commissioned a second lieutenant in the Delaware Army National Guard, eventually retiring as a full colonel in 1970. (Delaware Military Heritage and Education Foundation.)

Sgt. Phil Moore, Battery C, 261st Coast Artillery, stands outside the post exchange in the winter of 1941. On the right, Pvt. Bob Sterling, attending the radio school, stands by one of the 15-inch guns outside the post exchange in 1941. (Delaware Military Heritage and Education Foundation.)

Without a doubt, the most popular place on post to have a photograph taken was by the old 15-inch Rodman guns. Dozens of images exist like this one of Pat Davis, which was taken in 1942. The service hut (Building 126) appears in the background of the image. The building was used for many different purposes since being built in 1913. Bonnie Bonner said, "It was the site of the annual Halloween party for all us military kids. Also, where the monthly meetings of the American Legion Post No. 13 were held." Photographic evidence also suggests it was, at one time, used as a YMCA, post restaurant, and for various social functions. (Fort Delaware Society.)

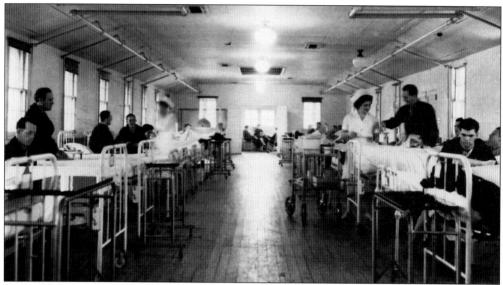

In January 1943, the *Fort DuPont Flashes* reported, "If surgery is required, patient is admitted to the surgical ward. The hospital is equipped with the most modern facilities ever produced by medical science for the treatment of illness. [On the right] Lt. H.W. Kipp, assisted by nurse, Miss Mastramino is changing a dressing on an operative incision on Pvt. Kenneth J. Boraton, 11th Infantry, West Dover, Md." (*Fort DuPont Flashes.*)

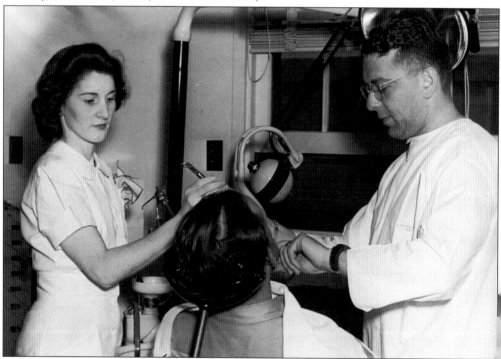

In the early 1940s, the original post hospital was converted to quarters for bachelor officers. Both dental and medical services were moved to the new station hospital in the cantonment area. Above, Lt. Charles Kovacs and an unknown nurse appear in the new dental wing of the station hospital. (Delaware Public Archives.)

The Quartermaster Corps (QMC) was responsible for respective fire departments on military posts across the country. These men, civilian contractors, even have QMC on their helmets. (Delaware Public Archives.)

An unknown civilian prepares to board a 1940s Chevrolet school bus (Admin 34) at Fort DuPont. During the war, buses drove routes from various military sites throughout the state. Automobile manufacturers did not update their car models during World War II and generally stuck with prewar styling until post-1946. The brick duplex (Building 90) in the background housed senior NCOs and families during the 1940s. (Delaware Public Archives.)

It is unknown where this photograph was taken, but the inside closely resembles one of the older buildings on post. By 1943, the post headquarters was moved to the old band barracks, which was larger and provided more office space. Above, a civilian clerk is shown doing inventory of assorted food stuffs ready for distribution. (Delaware Public Archives.)

Feeding the thousands of people at Fort DuPont was a serious endeavor. Here, Army cooks stand ready to serve a meal in one of the post mess halls. From left to right are, Pvt. Nat Kaysar, Pvt. Stefano Adda, Pvt. James McBride, Pvt. Louis Seligsohn, Pvt. Leon Friedman, Pvt. Arthur Week, and Cpl. Joseph Szymanski. (Photograph by Cpl. William O. King.)

Col. George Ruhlen and several soldiers appear in his office in early 1942. "Inauguration of War Bond Drive, Fort DuPont" is typed on the back of this photograph. From left to right are unidentified, Sgt. Albert Cinnamon, Sgt. Pat Mucci, Sgt. William Cohen, M.Sgt. Howard Atkinson, Pvt. Francis Burnett, Capt. W.A. Haviland (adjutant), Lt. Joseph Dixon (in charge of drive), and Colonel Ruhlen. Framed on the wall is the distinctive unit insignia (DUI) for the Harbor Defenses of the Delaware. (Fort Delaware Society.)

Near the post theater was a nine-hole golf course for use by the men and women at Fort DuPont. On May 15, 1942, there was an event called "Golf exhibition by pro golfers." Pictured from left to right are Sgt. Pat Mucci, Joe Kirkwood, Col. George Ruhlen, Ed Dudley, Jug McSpaden, Jimmy D'Angelo, and Leo Diegel. A 1942 issue of the *Fort DuPont Flashes* offers the opportunity for soldiers to take golf classes with Sgt. Pat Mucci, who took it upon himself to collect the equipment required. (Fort Delaware Society.)

On May 19, 1942, the Military Police Detachment (Local Security) is photographed on the parade field at Fort DuPont. Pictured here, from left to right, are (front row) Captain Reese, Ballard, Stillger, Reutty, Kahaniak, Vengen, Latterman, Abbond, R., Kern, Shevick, and Horvat; (second row) Casselberry, Mulcahey, Wechselberger, Casamenti, O'Neill, Moskowitz, Tobin, Hill, Ostendorf, and Klos; (third row) Sabatini, Gilligan, Nastasi, Feldstein, Alexander, Zitt, Gato, Register, Bayard, Abbond, W., and Beers; (fourth row) Poore, Bisher, Katz, Erwin, Zwirlein, Rogers, Minelli, and Nussbaum. (Photograph by Alex Siodmak.)

Capt. Edgar P. Reese, commanding the MP detachment, sits inside the headquarters building at Fort DuPont in 1942. His office is a typical example of other offices photographed on post. During the war, various military police units were at Fort DuPont, including the 26th MP Company, 101st MP Battalion, and 722nd MP Battalion. (Fort Delaware Society.)

Above, the 26th Infantry Division soldiers participate in a relay competition in 1942. The Yankee Division trained at Fort DuPont from October 9, 1942, until January 20 to 29, 1943. Individual units included the Headquarters Company, 101st Engineer Combat Battalion, 114th Medical Battalion, 26th Quartermaster Company, 39th Signal Repair Company, and the Special Training Unit for remedial training. (Delaware Public Archives.)

Besides the 26th Infantry Division (above), the XIII Army Corps trained in 1943. One of the XIII Corps was the 663rd Topographical Company. Pvt. Edward J. Haley (663rd) penned a few lines home on April 12, 1943. He wrote, "This is a little small post, you couldn't call it much more then a garrison, [and] they say it was built in the old days to protect Philadelphia. It's going to be ough for a while to get used to tough discipline again." (Delaware Public Archives.)

FORT DuPONT *Flashes*

Webb and Frye at work in the Salvage Warehouse

Pfc. Paul H. Purnell of Philadelphia served 11 months in the North African Theatre of Operations as part of a Quartermaster Trucking Regiment. This regiment was cited for night driving and delivering "Hot Stuff" to the front lines. Purnell can be seen at Fort Du Pont, driving safely in the cab of his truck with a smile on his face, as he thinks back on the times he drove under heavy enemy fire.

Pvt. J. Webb has been in the Army for three years. Did service in England with an outfit that did unloading and storing of important supplies for the Army Air Force. He tells of conditions when unceasing labor under heavy enemy air raids was necessary in order to get vitally needed supplies to their proper destination. Many a bomb he has handled has been sent to its proper destination by our Flying Fortresses. Here at Fort Du Pont, Webb still aids in the delivery of supplies to their proper destination, by working in the Salvage Warehouse.

Cpl. Jeff A. Williams comes originally from the state of South Carolina and prior to his entrance into the Army was studying for a degree in pharmacy at Duquesne University, Pittsburgh, Pa. He too, has foreign service, having landed in French Morocco with the Task Force that occupied Casablanca during the original landings in North Africa. Williams, while in North Africa, served with an ordnance company. During the final battle for Tunis and Bizerte, this company controlled the flow of ammunition that helped in driving the Germans out of North Africa. He prefers to forget the experiences of being bombed and strafed and proudly tells of his company having been selected as Guards of Honor for the President of the United States and his party, on one occasion during the Casablanca conferences. His company also holds the honor of having been selected to pass in review for the King of England because of meritous service during the final battle of North Africa. Cpl. Williams works here in the Training Division that gives aid in preparing men for overseas duty.

Cpl. Greene tuning up his motors.

Cpl. Williams is kept busy in the Training office.

Among the men who have not seen foreign service is Cpl. Harry C. Greene who spent eleven months in receiving and training of recruits at Camp Upton. Greene has since been transferred to the Ordnance Detachement here at Fort Du Pont, where he does his former civilian occupation efficiently as a motor mechanic. Greene is completely at home either snapping recruits to attention or tuning motors to "at ease".

Other men who have seen foreign service are Pvt. Rogers, North Africa and England, Pfc. Leroy Jones, England, and Pvt. Morgan, New Caladonia.

The *Fort DuPont Flashes* spotlights the soldiers of the 1231st Service Command Service Unit (SCSU) in the above article. Accordingly, "The Negro troops at Fort Du Pont are proud of the fact that almost half of them have seen action in one or two foreign theatre of operations. They have many interesting experiences to tell and feel that they are contributing directly to the wining of the war." One of the soldiers, Pfc. "Psycho" Sharpe, enlisted in the Army in 1941 and "spent nineteen months of his enlistment overseas in England and North Africa. While in North Africa his outfit was practically in contact with the enemy for seven months. Sharpe, who boasts of having prepared delicious meals for 'Old Blood and Guts' Patton, was injured during the battle for the Kasserine Pass and proudly wears his Purple Heart, which was pinned on him by General Roosevelt. He now prepares delicacies for the 1231st SCSU." (Photographs by Pvt. Michael Hollander.)

The 1st Chemical Decontamination Company (above) and the 99th Quartermaster Battalion were two African American units that trained at Fort DuPont during 1942 and 1943. The soldiers above wear the shoulder sleeve insignia of the Army Service Forces. On March 1, 1942, the 1st Chemical Company departed for overseas service. (Delaware Public Archives.)

Col. George Ruhlen pins a Good Conduct Medal on an African American soldier assigned to the 1231st Service Command at Fort DuPont. After 35 years of military service, Colonel Ruhlen retired from the US Army. In the summer of 1944, he was succeeded by Col. Randolph Russell as post commander. (Delaware Public Archives.)

On February 14, 1943, Colonel Ruhlen and Emma T. Ruhlen stand with giant paper hearts among soldiers and civilians. This image was likely taken in the recreation building (E-308) on Battery Lane. (Fort Delaware Society.)

The *Fort DuPont Flashes*, published by the Special Service Office, was located on post. The issues were a venue for morale and welfare during the war. This drawing is one of the more popular renditions, appearing in the September 1943 edition. (Sketch by Sgt. Reg. Webster.)

Here, a group of soldiers in work uniforms hold up the giant push ball near the flagstaff at Fort DuPont. Col. George Ruhlen is standing at the center of the group. A few lines on the back of the image state these soldiers are from the 261st Coast Artillery Battalion. (Fort Delaware Society.)

On August 6, 1943, Gov. Walter Bacon, the only mayor to be elected governor of Delaware, makes an appearance at Fort DuPont. Pictured from left to right are W.J. Farrell, Governor Bacon, Mrs. M.P. Farrell, Maj. Gen. Emil F. Reinhardt (XIII Corps), and Col. George Ruhlen. (Fort Delaware Society.)

Movie star Peggy Ann Garner signs autographs at Fort DuPont during the war. According to Mary Lou Monsen, "Every once in a while she would come down here and the whole place would go gaga because this movie star was coming." Her father, Lt. William H. Garner, was stationed at Fort DuPont and appears in the foreground. During the 1940s, Mary Lou Monsen lived with her family in the brick duplex (Building 90A) closest to the post exchange. Mary Lou's father was M.Sgt Ferdinand Monsen, who worked in the Quartermaster Detachment. (*Sunday Morning Star*.)

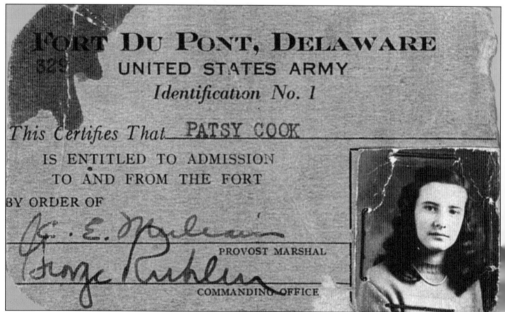

Due to heightened security, all civilians were required to have a signed pass to access the post. This identification card was issued to 13-year-old Patsy Cook, with the purpose of "Nurse–Mrs. E. L. Wittenborn" as typed on the reverse. The pass was issued on May 22, 1944. (Fort Delaware Society.)

In May 1944, soldiers from the Women's Army Corps arrived at the post. The *Fort DuPont Flashes* reports the post "has WACs on duty for the first time. So far only four have reported." Lt. Barbara J. Embre (above) attended the University of Iowa and served as president of the Zeta Tau Alpha Sorority. After college she worked for the R.C.A. Victor Company (Camden, New Jersey), which was where she left to join the WAC in October 1942. At Fort DuPont, she served as the assistant orientation officer and worked with Lt. Frederick Griffin Jr. (Delaware Public Archives.)

Before joining the Army, Lt. Helen J. Kraft (standing left) worked as a private secretary to her father who ran the Kraft Coal Company. While at Fort DuPont, she worked in the finance and fiscal office. Lieutenant Kraft, on recruiting duty, signed the "auburn-haired" Lt. Eula B. Toal (right). According to the *Fort DuPont Flashes*, Colonel Ruhlen assigned her "as personnel officer and assistant adjutant." (Delaware Public Archives.)

In mid-1944, guard towers and a barbed-wire fence were all erected around the cantonment barracks to serve as the 1265th SCSU prisoner of war camp. According to the *Fort DuPont Flashes* in May 1944, prison camp commander Lt. Col. John J. Harris was "already on duty here . . . making necessary advance arrangements." (National Archives.)

Leopold Gošnik, from Slovenia, was born on October 8, 1923. Due to his birth date, he was drafted into the German Army and was assigned to the 756th Gebirgsjäger (mountain-hunter), part of the 334th Gebirgs Division. According to Gošnik, his unit was sent to North Africa in December 1942. During Operation Vulcan, he was captured by the British Army on April 27, 1943. After three weeks as a captive, he sailed on the French ocean liner *Ille-de-France*, which arrived in the New York Harbor on July 6, 1943. He then took a three-day train bound for a POW camp in Roswell, New Mexico. In May 1944, Camp Roswell began to shut down, and Gošnik and other prisoners were transferred to Fort DuPont. He arrived on June 1, 1944, as part of the earliest documented reception of POWs. He worked at the officers' mess as a dishwasher and later as headwaiter. He was photographed wearing his Germany Army uniform while a POW in 1944. (Leopold Gošnik Collection.)

Two relief guards can be seen climbing the guard tower situated around the POW barracks. Four such towers were constructed around the complex to keep tabs on the prisoners. The barbed wire fence that surrounded the complex is barely visible on the far left. In November 1944, the International Red Cross reported, "The camp was established on May 24, the prisoners are [mostly] from Camp Roswell, New Mexico." On the day of the inspection, the number of prisoners included two medical officers, 17 NCOs, and 2,230 privates. Only 897 POWs were at Fort DuPont, the other 1,352 were divided among the five branch camps, located downstate. The base camp at Fort DuPont consisted of 23 two-story barracks, five mess halls and kitchens, four administration barracks, four recreation barracks, a guard barrack, barbershop, carpenter shop, laundry, canteen, paint shop, classroom, and large theater hall. Medical care consisted of an infirmary within the camp, while patients are treated at the station hospital outside of camp. (Photograph by Pvt. Michael Hollander.)

Here, German POWs are passing by the hospital near their barracks. Mary Lou Monsen said, "It was a prison, but we didn't call it that. We called it a barracks because we liked them. My grandmother use to bake pies and sit them out . . . on the window so that they could take them from the sun room." (Delaware Public Archives.)

Kurt Henkel appears in uniform while a member of the Deutsche Arbeitsfront (German Labor Front), an auxiliary force to the German Army. During the war, the Deutsche Arbeitsfront ran food, ammunition, and other necessities to frontline troops. By late war, six infantry battalions were formed. Henkel was captured on April 12, 1945, and sent by a liberty ship to the United States. A train took him from New York to his destination at Delaware City, where he arrived on May 1, 1945. While a POW, he worked in the hospital kitchen at the New Castle Army Air Field. During the war, POWs were employed at Fort DuPont as well as various off-post locations. On February 21, 1945, there were 44 separate work details totaling 653 POWs. On-post job sites included grounds, roads, coal yard, mess halls, commissary, post exchange, pumping plant, officers' club, and bakery. (Kurt Henkel Collection.)

German prisoners of war wearing "PW" marked on their uniforms still wear German Army headgear in this photograph, which was taken around 1944 or 1945. Kurt Henkel wrote, "I like to remember these days since I was treated well. I was still very young and celebrated my 17th birthday in the camp. I was lucky to be taken a US prisoner . . . and have thus been able to survive the war." (Delaware Public Archives.)

Pvt. Harry Hiemer, 1265th Military Police (Escort Guard), said of the prisoners of war, "The 1265th are most anxiously awaiting the new war prisoners. In fact, we are looking forward to their arrival with great anticipation. Wonder how the prisoners feel about it?" (Delaware State Parks.)

According to Mary Lou Monsen, "As children we were introduced to the German prisoners of war, and although the whole world was talking about these horrible, horrible people . . . we were seeing [them] as human beings and individuals." Including drive time, international regulations made it illegal for POWs to work more than 12-hours daily. Thus, branch camps were established closer to distant work sites, which included Henlopen Poultry (Lewes), Layton Lumber (Bridgeville), Buntings Nursery (Selbyville) and the Dover Airbase (officers' mess). There were even German POWs engaged in "repairing boardwalk" at Rehoboth Beach. (Delaware State Parks.)

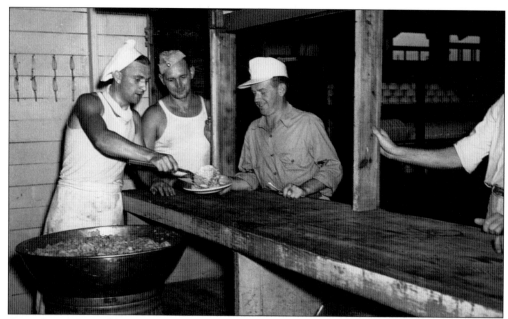

According to Leopold Gošnik, he "ate some dishes for the first time in his life in Fort DuPont, like cream soups, ice cream baked inside whipped eggs, and roast turkey. Boys working in the kitchen had an opportunity to serve themselves a beer or two occasionally, which their master sergeant benevolently overlooked. Leo found a secret hiding place under the shack's foundations for hidden reserves, even [hid] a whole box of beer, and once, two bottles of champagne." (Delaware Public Archives.)

Bernhard Freitag was captured by British troops on May 8, 1943. He wrote, "After having left the hell of Africa behind us the transfer to the US was a lot of fun." He spent two years as a POW before arriving at Fort DuPont in May 1945. According to Freitag, "It was still summer of 1945 when the commander of the camp selected four POWs to work in the camp commissary. Besides me there were a student from Berlin, called 'Moomps', who had excellent knowledge in English language so he additionally worked as a translator, Franz Eichinger from Lower Bavaria and Karl Latzl from Schlesien." At the commissary, he recalls working with four civilians: a man and three women. They are only remembered as Mr. "Happy" Holiday, Mrs. Burns, Alice, and Betty. He remembers other POWs mowing the lawn at Fort DuPont and sweeping the streets in Delaware City, which was popular because townspeople often gave them gifts. He added, "Afterwards we had spare time. It was used mainly by sports, reading or just being lazy. We played soccer or handball on the playground." (Bill Robelen Collection.)

Besides working elsewhere, POWs were employed throughout the post. Mary Lou Monsen said, "Two of them [Alex and Freddie] were working in our house and were implicitly entrusted with us." Above, Alex wears a Luftwaffe uniform while Freddie wears an issued shirt from the US Army. (Mary Lou Monsen-Evans Collection.)

A "Certificate of Credit Balance for Prisoner of War" documented the amount of money credited to individual POWs while in the United States. Form 19-70 shows Kurt Henkel had a balance of $41.50 on September 15, 1945. This document now lists the camp as the "1231st SCU PW Camp" which was another service command unit (written as SCU or SCSU) stationed at Fort DuPont. After the war, Henkel returned home to Frankfurt, Germany, spending many years working as a taxi driver. In 2006, he returned to Fort DuPont, this time for a visit, while on vacation traveling the country with his wife. (Delaware State Parks.)

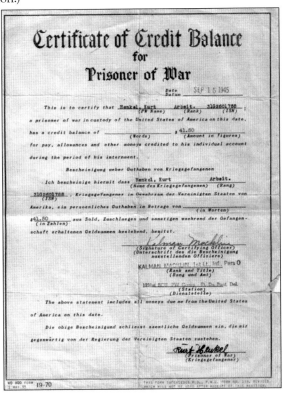

Lt. Col. John J. Harris served as the commanding officer of the prison camp at Fort DuPont. According to an inspection report, dated March 1, 1945, "The prisoners also desired the return of the caps which had been taken from them as a result of an incident several weeks previously in which regular issue materials had been cut up in order to make additional caps in the style of the Afrika Korps. The Camp Commander said that the caps would be returned but that they would all be dyed the same color." The report also mentions that Colonel Harris "inspects the branch camps twice a month and awards a green flag to the best camp which has exhibited the most progress [maintaining discipline] during the preceding several weeks." (Delaware State Parks.)

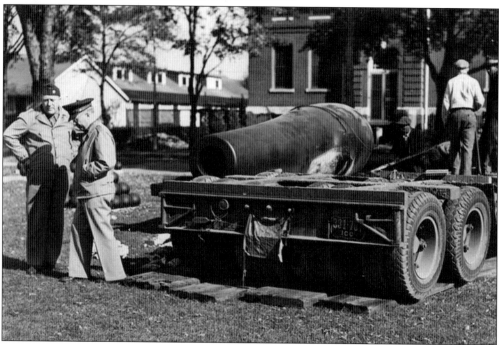

In 1944, the remaining armament at Fort DuPont, Fort Delaware, and Fort Mott were scrapped to support the war effort. Colonel Ruhlen (right) watched as the history of his beloved coast artillery slowly disappeared. Lt. Col. John J. O'Leary is the other officer in the photograph. (Andy Grant Collection.)

Five

ADAPT AND REUSE
1946–PRESENT

In the war's aftermath, Fort DuPont was declared surplus property and turned over to the state. The Governor Bacon Health Center was established in 1948, using the double company barracks as well as some of the houses and service buildings. Most of the frame mobilization buildings that were hastily constructed in wartime were torn down. The 285 total buildings that existed in 1943 now dwindled to less than 80.

In its new role as a hospital campus, the post still provided great memories for Delaware City residents. Martha Bennett fondly remembered playing softball and going to the theater. Kids in the 1970s visited Happy Hall, the roller rink that has since collapsed and been demolished. Chris McKinley recalled his childhood adventures, playing war and donning old military coats found in refuse piles near the river.

About 10 years after the health center took up residence, the old military post began to draw attention from concerned citizens. Newspaperman Bill Frank brought it to the limelight with newspaper articles touting its history. In June 1957, he ventured out to the site with a photographer to find "three youngsters, armed with wooden guns in their game of soldier, [keeping] the guard over the deserted gun emplacements." Frank's advocacy paid off, as others began to take an interest.

In 1976, the Delaware Army National Guard constructed an armory on site of the old POW camp, once again tying it to military service. The building was home station to the 736th Supply and Service Battalion and later to the 153rd Military Police Company.

Leah Roedel was one of those dedicated advocates who saw the value of the beautiful river site. At her urging in 1992, part of the post was transferred to the Delaware Department of Natural Resources and Environmental Control (DNREC), becoming Fort DuPont State Park. Four years later, the park was expanded to almost twice its size.

Citizens continue to advocate for adaptive reuse of historic Fort DuPont. Delaware State Parks has restored two of the brick NCO duplexes and performed stabilization on others. An ambitious residential curatorship program aims to save additional buildings through private partnership restoration initiatives. These efforts will hopefully help spur a coordinated effort on the part of all residential agencies to preserve Fort DuPont's historical legacy.

Built in 1930, the Delaware City Public School is located along Fifth Street by the old canal bridge. Fort DuPont and Delaware City children attended the school together. When the post was declared surplus and shut down, "DC" kids had to say farewell to their "Fort DuPonter" friends. In 2001, the school itself was closed and later reestablished as the Paul H. Morrill Jr. Library and Community Center. There, a large painting hangs on a wall that was rendered by "E. Klotsche," a German POW during the war. (University of Delaware.)

This 1950s photograph shows a truck passing over the old branch canal bridge that connects Delaware City to Fort DuPont. The bridge still stands today as part of Delaware Route 9. (Delaware Historical Society.)

After the war, Fort DuPont's buildings were adapted and reused to facilitate the 1948 opening of the Governor Bacon Health Center. It was dedicated by Dr. Mesrop A. Tarumianz as a "multi-health service center. It was named for Walter W. Bacon who had served as governor from 1940 to 1948." The main entrance was the main gate (Building 75) built by the Army decades before. It was eventually torn down to make way for the Reedy Point Bridge construction project in the 1960s. (Delaware Historical Society.)

Col. Joseph C. Mehaffey described the commanding officer's quarters as, "a fairly large brick house. On the first floor, in addition to the kitchen and butlers' pantry, there are a large central hall, two 15-foot-by-15-foot living rooms, and a dining room of about the same size. The second floor has three large bedrooms, two smaller rooms, and two bathrooms, and the third floor has two maids' rooms and a bathroom." In 1947, the house was modified as the health center's administration building. (Delaware Historical Society.)

MEDICAL CENTER, GOV. BACON HEALTH CENTER, DEL.
Photo by W. B. Nichols, Bristol, Pa.

Another repurposed building, the original band barracks also served as headquarters during World War II. Reusing Fort DuPont's buildings was a money-saving decision by the State of Delaware. The above building, maintained by a single budget, serves operational needs while simultaneously preserving cultural and natural resources. In October 1948, the state wrote, "This fine building is equipped with modern facilities, including operating rooms, X-ray and physiotherapy departments, clinical laboratory and pharmacy." (Delaware Historical Society.)

ELBERT B'LD'G. GOV. BACON HEALTH CENTER, DEL.
Photo by W. B Nichols, Bristol, Pa.

The Elbert Building, originally soldier barracks, was another building reused by the state. Sadly, all three framed barracks were demolished in the 1970s. The site currently serves as the main parking lot for the hospital. (Delaware Historical Society.)

Above, a 1950 Plymouth convertible is parked outside the Tilton Building, which still serves as the main hospital for the Governor Bacon Health Center. This building was originally the double-company barracks rebuilt in 1940. According to the Division of Public Health, the hospital provides "quality nursing care, medical treatment, social service, activity therapy, and physical therapy for the long-term care needs of [over 90] residents." (Delaware Historical Society.)

Built in 1932, the swimming pool had a shallow depth of two feet which gradually descended to eight feet. There were concrete stairs in the shallow end and a metal ladder in the deep end. During the 1950s to 1970s, the pool was opened to residents and all of Delaware City. By the 1990s, the pool was empty and eventually was filled in. (Delaware Historical Society.)

In 1951, the State Civil Defense established, in the abandoned mortar batteries, a temporary field headquarters primarily used during statewide training exercises. In February 1956, following major renovations, the batteries opened as the full-time headquarters for the State Division of Civil Defense. (Fort Delaware Society.)

The space was renovated "into an office suite with about 10,000 square feet of floor space, [and] the blast and radiation proof installation now is a modern civil defense control center," according to the History of the Delaware Emergency Operations Center. (Fort Delaware Society.)

According to the state, "Major features of the renovations were the revamping of the entire electrical system, installation of a dehumidification system, sanitary facilities, and water piping. More recent additions [during the 1960s-1970s] include the installation of its own automatic emergency power generator and underground water supply, carpeting, status boards, PA system, and computer area." (Fort Delaware Society.)

The wall inset, for auxiliary lights, is the only reference point establishing this as the gallery inside the mortar batteries. When the Cold War ended, so did the interest in using the operations center. During the 1990s, it was used for storage, but the irregular water table further discouraged any use of the "bunker." (Fort Delaware Society.)

In 1984, Fort Delaware Society members were afforded an opportunity to explore Batteries Read and Gibson. Only fragments of tar weatherproofing remain, while invasive species begin to overtake the emplacements in this photograph. Fort DuPont's gun batteries have suffered greatly from the lack of funding, which is sorely needed for basic care and maintenance. (Fort Delaware Society.)

Battery Best's power station was modified during the 1950s to support the civil defense emergency generator. In the photograph, visitors climb stairs to the top of the mortar batteries. Currently, this area is overgrown and the stairs are in disrepair. Bonnie Bonner said, "As we drove around the post, I was literally shocked to see the dilapidated condition of many of the remaining buildings. My initial thoughts were of how much history was being lost by such disregard for proper maintenance!" (Fort Delaware Society.)

On March 4, 1992, Delawareans gather inside the theater to witness the birth of Fort DuPont State Park. Dr. Edwin Clark, secretary of DNREC, is speaking at the podium. Gov. Michael N. Castle is seated on the left, next to Tom Eichler, secretary of DHSS. Leah Roedel, the lobbyist responsible for establishment of the park, is seated on the right. (Photograph by Bill Craven.)

Fort DuPont's legacy was slowing being destroyed until she stepped in. Leah Roedel (right) lobbied for almost 10 years to get the fort established as a state park. According to park superintendent Becky Webb, "She knew exactly what she needed to do and needed to say, and people listened to her." During her time on the Parks Advisory Council, she helped establish at least eight state parks in Delaware. In May 1992, she was honored with the Delaware Audubon Conservation Award. William J. Hopkins, director of Delaware State Parks, is pictured with Roedel. Photograph by Bill Craven.)

In 2005, the quartermaster office (Building 113) stands in an abandoned state following reuse by the health center. The following year, the Fort Delaware Society, 501(c)(3) nonprofit organization, completed the stabilization and rehabilitation of the structure becoming the first successful partner in Delaware State Parks' curatorship program. (Photograph by Bill Robelen.)

In May 2007, the 153rd Military Police Company was federally mobilized in support of Operation Iraqi Freedom. In the photograph above and during June 2007, soldiers of the unit formed a mass formation on the parade field during a deployment ceremony. Note the Tilton Building (double company barracks) on the left. (Delaware Army National Guard.)

Calvin Duker and Chris McKinley (right) are both longtime employees of the health center. In April 2011, they appear outside of the original carpenter shop (Building 61), which is still being used by the state. The structure was built in 1916 following standard plan No. 53. (Photograph by Brendan Mackie.)

In March 2011, visitors stand outside the former commanding officer's quarters at Fort DuPont. Although, the beautiful porch is long gone, the building still functions as the headquarters for the Governor Bacon Health Center. The house was built in 1910, following standard plan No. 35. (Photograph by Brendan Mackie.)

In fall 2009, the Delaware Military Heritage and Education Foundation held the first Delaware Military Weekend at Fort DuPont. Although the theater is still vacant, the state allotted funds for stabilization. In 2007, a new roof was installed, and the marquee was restored. (Photograph by Laura M. Lee.)

On June 5, 2011, Col. James Begley presents Capt. Daniel DeFlaviis and 1st Sgt. Jerold Huber with the Iraq campaign battle streamer for their service overseas. In the background, Sgt. Brandon Kelly holds the guidon. This presentation took place outside the Maj. Gen. Joseph J. Scannel Armory, built in 1976 and located on the exact site of the former POW camp. (Photograph by Sgt. James Pernol; 101st Public Affairs Detachment.)

Tom Smith, a history buff and state park employee, is dedicated to the preservation and maintenance work at Fort DuPont. Above, Smith stands along Maple Boulevard (now Sussex Avenue), which is a short distance from Quarters 22, where the Bonner family once lived. (Photograph by Brendan Mackie.)

During the summer months, invasive species and thick underbrush essentially render the Twenty Gun Battery unrecognizable. (Photograph by Brendan Mackie.)

Maia Julia Lee and Simba pass the boarded up guardhouse while on a walk at Fort DuPont. Accordin to Delaware State Parks, this is the next building slated for restoration. Bonnie Bonner Rorabaug wrote, "Moving back to Delaware and visiting the fort in 2004, I was deeply saddened by the loss so many beautiful buildings once gracing the streets of that Army installation. Buildings that he so many memories for so many people. And now, gone! Buildings, that if they had voices, wou mesmerize us with tales of bygone days. The history of not only the military personnel but also the families—wives and children—and how they lived and thrived and enjoyed being part of a milita environment." (Photograph by Brendan Mackie.)

Jim Campo and several whippets appear above during a race weekend in 2011. According to Jir the Jersey Rag Racers have been using the recreation space since the early 1980s. Other nonprof organizations like the Kirkwood Soccer Club and Civil Air Patrol also use the site regularl (Photograph by Brendan Mackie.)

In November 2010, Brett Truitt shovels years' worth of leaves from Battery Elder's emplacement No. 1. Elder is in surprisingly good condition despite decades of neglect. The restoration and maintenance has primarily been accomplished by volunteer groups along with dedicated park employees. (Photograph by Brendan Mackie.)

ke Miller and Sarah Ferguson are shown hard at work clearing debris from behind Battery Elder preparation for upcoming tours. (Photograph by Brendan Mackie.)

Tracy Walters (left) and Pedro "Mike" Almeida, both Fort DuPont State Park grounds employees, pause after clearing invasive trees from Battery Elder's slope. Trees and underbrush growing on the gun batteries can cause serious structural damage to the concrete and an instigating factor in sink holes. (Photograph by Brendan Mackie.)

Bank of America volunteers gather behind Battery Elder following a cleanup day in March 2011. Volunteer groups are instrumental in preservation and restoration efforts at Fort DuPont State Park. (Photograph by Brendan Mackie.)

BIBLIOGRAPHY

Ames, David L., Dean A. Doerrfeld, Allison W. Elterich, Caroline C. Fisher, and Rebecca J. Siders. *Fort DuPont, Delaware: An Architectural Survey and Evaluation.* Newark, DE: University of Delaware, Center for Historic Architecture and Engineering, 1994.

Berhow, Mark A. *American Seacoast Defenses, A Reference Guide.* Bel Air, MD: CDSG Press, 1999.

Contant, George. *Oral History Interview: Mary Lou Monsen-Evans.* Dover, DE: Delaware State Parks, Cultural Resource Unit, 2010.

Crumrine, Bishop. "Letters Sent 1862–1865." Washington and Jefferson College, U. Grant Miller Library, January 2005.

Duncan, William H. *261st Cost Artillery Battalion (Harbor Defense).* Wilmington, DE: Delaware Military Heritage and Education Foundation, 2000.

Federal Writers' Project of the Works Progress Administration. *Delaware: A Guide to the First State.* New York, NY: The Viking Press, 1938.

Frank, William P. "Weeds, Three Boys Playing Soldier Take Over at Forgotten Fort DuPont." *Wilmington Morning News,* June 28, 1957: 33.

Gaines, William C. "The Coastal and Harbor Defenses of the Delaware, Part III." *Coast Defense Study Group Journal,* vol. 10, no. 2 (May 1996): 19–72.

Gillespie, A. G. *A Guide to Coast Artillery Posts.* Walworth, WI: Walworth Times Print, 1915.

Hamilton, Alexander J. *A Fort Delaware Journal: The Diary of a Yankee Private, A.J. Hamilton, 1862–1865.* W. Emerson Wilson, ed. Wilmington, DE: Fort Delaware Society, 1981.

Harper's New Monthly Magazine. "Among the Peaches." New York, NY: Harper & Brothers, 1870.

Heimer, Harry. "Hits and Bits of the 1265th." *Fort DuPont Flashes,* June–July 1944: 20–11.

Henkel, Kurt. "Thanksgiving 1945 in the POW Camp Fort DuPont." Hamburg, Germany: Kurt Henkel, 2010.

Lewis, Neil. "Childhood Memories of Fort DuPont 1933 to 1939." *Fort Delaware Notes,* vol. 60 (2010): 45–48 .

Nowland, Jacob. "Willie Blum, German POW at Fort DuPont." Delaware City, DE: Fort DuPont State Park, 2010.

Philadelphia Inquirer. "A Ten Gun Battery on the Delaware River." November 7, 1863: 4.

Philadelphia Inquirer. "Wilmington Draft to Ft. DuPont." October 22, 1918: 11.

Raphael, R. J., "Complement Gab." *Fort DuPont Flashes,* May 1944: 5-8.

Ruhlen, George. "Personal Correspondence 1940–1944." Delaware City, DE: Fort Delaware Society, 2010.

Santeramo, Ralph J., *My Years in the United States Army: January 25, 1941–December 8, 1945.* San Diego, CA: Ralph J. Santeramo, 2006.

Springer, Willard., Leland Lyon, C. J. Prickett, James Beebe, Dorsey W. Lewis, Earl M. Tull, William R. Murray, Thomas W. Murray, and George M. Fisher. "Third Biennial Report of the State Board of Trustees of the Governor Bacon Health Center at Delaware City, Delaware." Dover, DE: State of Delaware, 1955.

Sunday Morning Star. "WPA Constructs Building in 12 Days as Part Of Fort DuPont's Modernization Program." *The Sunday Morning Star,* May 26, 1940: 1.

Tršinar, Irena. "Leopold Gošnik: A Prisoner of War at Fort DuPont, 1944–1945," *Fort Delaware Notes,* vol. 58 (2007): 18–26.

Williamson, Peter, D. Andrew Pitz, Richard Sprenkle, and Steven Kuter. *Conceptual Master Plan: Fort DuPont State Park, Delaware City, Delaware.* Media, PA: Natural Lands Trust, 1995.

Williford, Glen. "American Seacoast Defense Sites of the 1870s, Part II, Delaware River–San Francisco." *Coast Defense Journal,* vol. 21, no. 4 (November 2007): 59–110.

www.arcadiapublishing.com

MAP SEARCH

Discover books about the town where you grew up, the cities where your friends and families live, the town where your parents met, or even that retirement spot you've been dreaming about. Our Web site provides history lovers with exclusive deals, advanced notification about new titles, e-mail alerts of author events, and much more.

Arcadia Publishing, the leading local history publisher in the United States, is committed to making history accessible and meaningful through publishing books that celebrate and preserve the heritage of America's people and places. Consistent with our mission to preserve history on a local level, this book was printed in South Carolina on American-made paper and manufactured entirely in the United States.

Find Your Place in History.